# THE LITTLE CLAY CART
## (MRCCHAKATIKA)

# THE LITTLE CLAY CART
## (MRCCHAKATIKA)
## A HINDU DRAMA,
## ATTRIBUTED TO KING SHUDRAKA

TRANSLATED FROM THE ORIGINAL SANSKRIT AND PRAKRITS

INTO ENGLISH PROSE AND VERSE

ARTHUR WILLIAM RYDER

GYAN

*Published by*

GYAN

Gyan Publishing House
5, Ansari Road
Daryaganj, New Delhi-110002
Phone: 011-47034999, 9811692060
E-mail: books@gyanbooks.com

*Distribution Network*
gyanbooks.com
India, USA, Canada, UK, Australia



ISBN: 978-93-7097-069-4 (HB)
First Published, 1905

2nd Impression 2025

*Printed at:* Gyan Press, Delhi.



**THE LITTLE CLAY CART (MRCCHAKATIKA)**
Arthur ARTHUR WILLIAM RYDER

THE HARVARD ORIENTAL SERIES

VOLUME NINE

# HARVARD ORIENTAL SERIES

EDITED
WITH THE COÖPERATION OF VARIOUS SCHOLARS
BY
CHARLES ROCKWELL LANMAN
WALES PROFESSOR OF SANSKRIT IN HARVARD UNIVERSITY

## Volume Nine

CAMBRIDGE, MASSACHUSETTS
Published by Harvard University
1905

# THE LITTLE CLAY CART

[MṚCCHAKAṬIKA]

## A Hindu Drama

ATTRIBUTED TO KING SHŪDRAKA

TRANSLATED FROM THE ORIGINAL SANSKRIT AND PRĀKRITS

INTO ENGLISH PROSE AND VERSE

BY

ARTHUR WILLIAM RYDER, PH.D.

INSTRUCTOR IN SANSKRIT IN HARVARD UNIVERSITY

CAMBRIDGE, MASSACHUSETTS

Published by Harvard University

1905

TO MY FATHER

WILLIAM HENRY RYDER

# CONTENTS

## NOTE BY THE EDITOR

W*ITH the battle of the Sea of Japan another turning-point in the brief course of recorded human history has been reached. Whatever the outcome of the negotiations for peace, one thing is sure: for better, for worse, and whether we will or no, the West must know the East, and the East must know the West. With that knowledge will inevitably come an interchange of potent influences, of influences that will affect profoundly the religion and morals, the philosophy, the literature, the art, in short, all the elements that make up the civilizations of the two hemispheres. It is a part of the responsibility resting upon the molders and leaders of the thought and life of our time, and upon our Universities in particular, to see to it that these new forces, mighty for good or for evil, are directed aright.*

*The fruitfulness of those scions of Western civilization which the Japanese have grafted upon their own stock is to-day the admiration of the world. In our wonder, let us not forget that that stock is the growth of centuries, and that it is rooted in a soil of racial character informed by ethical ideals which we are wont to regard, with arrogant self-complacency, as exclusively proper to Christianity, but which were, in fact, inculcated twenty-four centuries ago through precept and example by Gotama the Enlightened, or, as the Hindus called him, Gotama the Buddha. It has often been said that India has never influenced the development of humanity as a whole. Be that as it may, it now seems no less probable than strange that she is yet destined to do so, on the one hand, indirectly, through the influence of Indian Buddhism upon Japan, and, on the other, directly, by the diffusion in the West of a knowledge of her sacred writings, espe-*

*cially those of Vedantism and Buddhism. To judge the East aright, we must know not only what she is, but also how she has become what she is; know, in short, some of the principal phases of her spiritual history as they are reflected in her ancient literature, especially that of India. To interpret to the West the thought of the East, to bring her best and noblest achievements to bear upon our life,—that is to-day the problem of Oriental philology.*

*The Harvard Oriental Series embodies an attempt to present to Western scholars, in trustworthy texts and translations, some of the greatest works of the Hindu literature and philosophy and religion, together with certain instruments, such as the Vedic Concordance or the History of the Beast-fable, for their critical study or elucidation. Some account of the volumes completed or in progress may be found at the end of this book. Dr. Ryder, passing by for the present the more momentous themes of religion and philosophy, has in this volume attempted to show what the Indian genius, in its strength and in its weakness, could do in the field of literature pure and simple. The timeliness of the Series as a whole is an eloquent tribute to the discernment of my loved and unforgotten pupil and friend, Henry Clarke Warren. In him were united not only the will and the ability to establish such a publication as this, but also the learning and insight which enabled him to forecast in a general way its possibilities of usefulness. He knew that the East had many a lesson to teach the West; but whether the lesson be repose of spirit or hygiene of the soldier in the field, whether it be the divine immanence or simplicity of life or the overcoming of evil with good, he knew that the first lesson to be taught us was the teachable habit of mind.*

C. R. L.

June, 1905

# PREFACE

THE text chosen as the basis of this translation is that given in the edition of Parab,[1] and I have chosen it for the following reasons. Parab's edition is the most recent, and its editor is a most admirable Sanskrit scholar, who, it seems to me, has in several places understood the real meaning of the text better than his predecessors. This edition contains the comment of Pṛthvīdhara; it is far freer from misprints than many texts printed in India, and, in respect to arrangement and typography, it is clear and convenient. Besides, it is easily obtainable and very cheap. This last consideration may prove to be of importance, if the present translation should be found helpful in the class-room. For the sake of cataloguers, I note that the proper transliteration of the Sanskrit names of this title according to the rules laid down by the American Library Association in its Journal for 1885, is as follows: Mṛcchakaṭika; Çūdraka; Pṛthvīdhara; Kāçīnātha Pāṇḍurañga Paraba; Nirṇaya-Sāgara.

The verse-numeration of each act follows the edition of Parab; fortunately, it is almost identical with the numeration in the editions of Godabole and Jīvānanda. For the convenience of those who may desire to consult this book in connection with Stenzler's edition, I have added references at the top of the page to that edition as well as to the edition of Parab. In these references, the letter P. stands for Parab, the letter S. for Stenzler.

There are a few passages in which I have deviated from Parab's text. A list of such passages is given on page 177. From this list

[1] The Mṛichchhakaṭika of Śūdraka with the commentary of Pṛithvīdhara. Edited by Kāshināth Pāṇḍurang Parab. Bombay: Nirṇaya-Sāgar Press. 1900. Price 1 Rupee. It may be had of O. Harrassowitz in Leipzig for 2½ Marks.

I have omitted a few minor matters, such as slight misprints and what seem to me to be errors in the *chāyā;* these matters, and the passages of unusual interest or difficulty, I shall treat in a series of notes on the play, which I hope soon to publish in the Journal of the American Oriental Society. It is hardly necessary to give reasons for the omission of the passage inserted by Nīlakaṇṭha in the tenth act (Parab, 288.3–292.9). This passage is explicitly declared by tradition to be an interpolation by another hand, and it is clearly shown to be such by internal evidence. It will be noticed that the omission of this passage causes a break in the verse-numeration of the tenth act, where the verse-number 54 is followed by the number 58.

Of the books which have been useful to me in the present work, I desire to mention especially the editions of Stenzler, Godabole, Jīvānanda Vidyāsāgara, and Parab; the commentaries of Pṛthvīdhara, Lallādīkṣita, and Jīvānanda; further, the translations of Wilson, Regnaud, and Böhtlingk.

A number of friends were kind enough to read my manuscript, and each contributed something. I wish to mention especially my friend and pupil, Mr. Walter E. Clark, of Harvard University, whose careful reading of both text and translation was fruitful of many good suggestions.

But by far my greatest personal indebtedness is to Professor Lanman, whose generous interest in my work has never flagged from the day when I began the study of Sanskrit under his guidance. He has criticized this translation with the utmost rigor; indeed, the pages are few which have not witnessed some improvement from his hand. It is to him also that I owe the accuracy and beauty which characterize the printed book; nothing has been hard enough to weary him, nothing small enough to escape him.

And more than all else, I am grateful to him for the opportunity of publishing in the Harvard Oriental Series; for this series is that enterprise which, since the death of Professor Whitney, most honorably upholds in this country the standards of accurate scholarship set by the greatest of American Sanskritists.

ARTHUR W. RYDER

*Harvard University*
*May 23, 1905*

# INTRODUCTION

## I. THE AUTHOR AND THE PLAY

CONCERNING the life, the date, and the very identity[1] of King Shūdraka, the reputed author of The Little Clay Cart, we are curiously ignorant. No other work is ascribed to him, and we have no direct information about him, beyond the somewhat fanciful statements of the Prologue to this play. There are, to be sure, many tales which cluster about the name of King Shūdraka, but none of them represents him as an author. Yet our very lack of information may prove, to some extent at least, a disguised blessing. For our ignorance of external fact compels a closer study of the text, if we would find out what manner of man it was who wrote the play. And the case of King Shūdraka is by no means unique in India; in regard to every great Sanskrit writer,—so bare is Sanskrit literature of biography,—we are forced to concentrate attention on the man as he reveals himself in his works. First, however, it may be worth while to compare Shūdraka with two other great dramatists of India, and thus to discover, if we may, in what ways he excels them or is excelled by them.

Kālidāsa, Shūdraka, Bhavabhūti—assuredly, these are the greatest names in the history of the Indian drama. So different are these men, and so great, that it is not possible to assert for any one of them such supremacy as Shakspere holds in the English drama. It is true that Kālidāsa's dramatic masterpiece, the Shakuntalā, is the most widely known of the Indian plays. It is true that the tender and elegant Kālidāsa has been called, with a not wholly for-

[1] For an illuminating discussion of these matters, the reader is referred to Sylvain Lévi's admirable work, Le Théâtre Indien, Paris, 1890, pages 196–211.

tunate enthusiasm, the "Shakspere of India." But this rather exclusive admiration of the Shakuntalā results from lack of information about the other great Indian dramas. Indeed, it is partly due to the accident that only the Shakuntalā became known in translation at a time when romantic Europe was in full sympathy with the literature of India.

Bhavabhūti, too, is far less widely known than Kālidāsa; and for this the reason is deeper-seated. The austerity of Bhavabhūti's style, his lack of humor, his insistent grandeur, are qualities which prevent his being a truly popular poet. With reference to Kālidāsa, he holds a position such as Aeschylus holds with reference to Euripides. He will always seem to minds that sympathize with his grandeur[1] the greatest of Indian poets; while by other equally discerning minds of another order he will be admired, but not passionately loved.

Yet however great the difference between Kālidāsa, "the grace of poetry,"[2] and Bhavabhūti, "the master of eloquence,"[3] these two authors are far more intimately allied in spirit than is either of them with the author of The Little Clay Cart. Kālidāsa and Bhavabhūti are Hindus of the Hindus; the Shakuntalā and the Latter Acts of Rāma could have been written nowhere save in India: but Shūdraka, alone in the long line of Indian dramatists, has a cosmopolitan character. Shakuntalā is a Hindu maid, Mādhava is a Hindu hero; but Sansthānaka and Maitreya and Madanikā are citizens of the world. In some of the more striking characteristics of Sanskrit literature—in its fondness for system, its elaboration of style, its love of epigram—Kālidāsa and Bhavabhūti are far truer

[1] In his Mālatīmādhava, i. 8, he says: "Whoever they may be who now proclaim their contempt for me, —they know something, but *this* work was not for them. Yet there will arise a man of nature like mine own; for time is endless, and the world is wide." This seems prophetic of John Milton. [2] Prasannarāghava, i. 22. [3] Mahāvīracarita, i. 4.

to their native land than is Shūdraka. In Shūdraka we find few of those splendid phrases in which, as the Chinese[1] say, "it is only the words which stop, the sense goes on,"—phrases like Kālidāsa's[2] "there are doors of the inevitable everywhere," or Bhavabhūti's[3] "for causeless love there is no remedy." As regards the predominance of swift-moving action over the poetical expression of great truths, The Little Clay Cart stands related to the Latter Acts of Rāma as Macbeth does to Hamlet. Again, Shūdraka's style is simple and direct, a rare quality in a Hindu; and although this style, in the passages of higher emotion, is of an exquisite simplicity, yet Shūdraka cannot infuse into mere language the charm which we find in Kālidāsa or the majesty which we find in Bhavabhūti.

Yet Shūdraka's limitations in regard to stylistic power are not without their compensation. For love of style slowly strangled originality and enterprise in Indian poets, and ultimately proved the death of Sanskrit literature. Now just at this point, where other Hindu writers are weak, Shūdraka stands forth preëminent. Nowhere else in the hundreds of Sanskrit dramas do we find such variety, and such drawing of character, as in The Little Clay Cart; and nowhere else, in the drama at least, is there such humor. Let us consider, a little more in detail, these three characteristics of our author; his variety, his skill in the drawing of character, his humor.

To gain a rough idea of Shūdraka's variety, we have only to recall the names of the acts of the play. Here The Shampooer who Gambled and The Hole in the Wall are shortly followed by The Storm; and The Swapping of the Bullock-carts is closely succeeded by The Strangling of Vasantasenā. From farce to tragedy, from

[1] History of Chinese Literature, by H. A. Giles, pages 145–146.

[2] Shakuntalā, i. 15.

[3] Latter Acts of Rāma, v. 17.

satire to pathos, runs the story, with a breadth truly Shaksperian. Here we have philosophy:

*The lack of money is the root of all evil.* (*i. 14*)

And pathos:

*My body wet by tear-drops falling, falling;*
*My limbs polluted by the clinging mud;*
*Flowers from the graveyard torn, my wreath appalling;*
*For ghastly sacrifice hoarse ravens calling,*
*And for the fragrant incense of my blood.* (*x. 3*)

And nature description:

*But mistress, do not scold the lightning. She is your friend,*
*This golden cord that trembles on the breast*
*Of great Airāvata; upon the crest*
*Of rocky hills this banner all ablaze;*
*This lamp in Indra's palace; but most blest*
*As telling where your most belovèd stays.* (*v. 33*)

And genuine bitterness:

*Pride and tricks and lies and fraud*
*Are in your face;*
*False playground of the lustful god,*
*Such is your face;*
*The wench's stock in trade, in fine,*
*Epitome of joys divine,*
*I mean your face—*
*For sale! the price is courtesy.*
*I trust you'll find a man to buy*
*Your face.* (*v. 36*)

It is natural that Shūdraka should choose for the expression of matters so diverse that type of drama which gives the greatest scope to the author's creative power. This type is the so-called "drama of invention,"[1] a category curiously subordinated in India to the heroic drama, the plot of which is drawn from history or mythology. Indeed, The Little Clay Cart is the only extant drama which fulfils the spirit of the drama of invention, as defined by the Sanskrit canons of dramaturgy. The plot of the "Mālatī and Mādhava," or of the "Mallikā and Māruta," is in no true sense the invention of the author; and The Little Clay Cart is the only drama of invention which is "full of rascals."[2]

But a spirit so powerful as that of King Shūdraka could not be confined within the strait-jacket of the minute, and sometimes puerile, rules of the technical works. In the very title of the drama, he has disregarded the rule[3] that the name of a drama of invention should be formed by compounding the names of heroine and hero.[4] Again, the books prescribe[5] that the hero shall appear in every act; yet Chārudatta does not appear in acts ii., iv., vi., and viii. And further, various characters, Vasantasenā, Maitreya, the courtier, and others, have vastly gained because they do not conform too closely to the technical definitions.

The characters of The Little Clay Cart are living men and women. Even when the type makes no strong appeal to Western minds, as in the case of Chārudatta, the character lives, in a sense in which Dushyanta[6] or even Rāma[7] can hardly be said to live. Shūdraka's men are better individualized than his women; this fact alone differentiates him sharply from other Indian dramatists. He draws on every class of society, from the high-souled Brahman to the executioner and the housemaid.

His greatest character is unquestionably Sansthānaka, this com-

[1] *Prakaraṇa.* [2] *Dhūrtasaṁkula:* Daçarūpa, iii. 38. [3] *Sāhityadarpaṇa*, 428.
[4] As in Mālatī-mādhava. [5] Daçarūpa, iii. 33. [6] In Kālidāsa's Shakuntalā.
[7] In Bhavabhūti's Latter Acts of Rāma.

bination of ignorant conceit, brutal lust, and cunning, this greater than Cloten, who, after strangling an innocent woman, can say:[1] "Oh, come! Let's go and play in the pond." Most attractive characters are the five[2] conspirators, men whose home is "east of Suez and the ten commandments." They live from hand to mouth, ready at any moment to steal a gem-casket or to take part in a revolution, and preserving through it all their character as gentlemen and their irresistible conceit. And side by side with them moves the hero Chārudatta, the Buddhist beau-ideal of manhood,

*A tree of life to them whose sorrows grow,*
*Beneath its fruit of virtue bending low.* (*i. 48*)

To him, life itself is not dear, but only honor.[3] He values wealth only as it supplies him with the means of serving others. We may, with some justice, compare him with Antonio in The Merchant of Venice. There is some inconsistency, from our point of view, in making such a character the hero of a love-drama; and indeed, it is Vasantasenā who does most of the love-making.[4]

Vasantasenā is a character with neither the girlish charm of Shakuntalā[5] nor the mature womanly dignity of Sītā.[6] She is more admirable than lovable. Witty and wise she is, and in her love as true as steel; this too, in a social position which makes such constancy difficult. Yet she cannot be called a great character; she does not seem so true to life as her clever maid, Madanikā. In making the heroine of his play a courtezan, Shūdraka follows a suggestion of the technical works on the drama; he does not thereby cast any imputation of ill on Vasantasenā's character. The courtezan class in India corresponded roughly to the hetæræ of

[1] See page 128.
[2] Aryaka, Darduraka, Chandanaka, Sharvilaka, and the courtier.
[3] See x. 27.
[4] See v. 46 and the following stage-direction.
[5] In Kālidāsa's play of that name.
[6] In Bhavabhūti's Latter Acts of Rāma.

ancient Greece or the geishas of Japan; it was possible to be a courtezan and retain one's self-respect. Yet the inherited[1] way of life proves distasteful to Vasantasenā; her one desire is to escape its limitations and its dangers by becoming a legal wife.[2]

In Maitreya, the Vidūshaka, we find an instance of our author's masterly skill in giving life to the dry bones of a rhetorical definition. The Vidūshaka is a stock character who has something in common with a jester; and in Maitreya the essential traits of the character—eagerness for good food and other creature comforts, and blundering devotion to his friend—are retained, to be sure, but clarified and elevated by his quaint humor and his readiness to follow Chārudatta even in death. The grosser traits of the typical Vidūshaka are lacking. Maitreya is neither a glutton nor a fool, but a simple-minded, whole-hearted friend.

The courtier is another character suggested by the technical works, and transformed by the genius of Shūdraka. He is a man not only of education and social refinement, but also of real nobility of nature. But he is in a false position from the first, this true gentleman at the wretched court of King Pālaka; at last he finds the courage to break away, and risks life, and all that makes life attractive, by backing Aryaka. Of all the conspirators, it is he who runs the greatest risk. To his protection of Vasantasenā is added a touch of infinite pathos when we remember that he was himself in love with her.[3] Only when Vasantasenā leaves him[4] without a thought, to enter Chārudatta's house, does he realize how much he loves her; then, indeed, he breaks forth in words of the most passionate jealousy. We need not linger over the other characters, except to observe that each has his marked individuality,

[1] See viii. 43. [2] See pages 65–66 and page 174.

[3] See viii. 38; and compare the words, "Yet love bids me prattle," on page 86. [4] Page 87.

and that each helps to make vivid this picture of a society that seems at first so remote.

Shūdraka's humor is the third of his vitally distinguishing qualities. This humor has an American flavor, both in its puns and in its situations. The plays on words can seldom be adequately reproduced in translation, but the situations are independent of language. And Shūdraka's humor runs the whole gamut, from grim to farcical, from satirical to quaint. Its variety and keenness are such that King Shūdraka need not fear a comparison with the greatest of Occidental writers of comedies.

It remains to say a word about the construction of the play. Obviously, it is too long. More than this, the main action halts through acts ii. to v., and during these episodic acts we almost forget that the main plot concerns the love of Vasantasenā and Chārudatta. Indeed, we have in The Little Clay Cart the material for two plays. The larger part of act i. forms with acts vi. to x. a consistent and ingenious plot; while the remainder of act i. might be combined with acts iii. to v. to make a pleasing comedy of lighter tone. The second act, clever as it is, has little real connection either with the main plot or with the story of the gems. The breadth of treatment which is observable in this play is found in many other specimens of the Sanskrit drama, which has set itself an ideal different from that of our own drama. The lack of dramatic unity and consistency is often compensated, indeed, by lyrical beauty and charms of style; but it suggests the question whether we might not more justly speak of the Sanskrit plays as dramatic poems than as dramas. In The Little Clay Cart, at any rate, we could ill afford to spare a single scene, even though the very richness and variety of the play remove it from the class of the world's greatest dramas.

## II. THE TRANSLATION

The following translation is sufficiently different from previous translations of Indian plays to require a word of explanation. The difference consists chiefly in the manner in which I have endeavored to preserve the form of the original. The Indian plays are written in mingled prose and verse; and the verse portion forms so large a part of the whole that the manner in which it is rendered is of much importance. Now this verse is not analogous to the iambic trimeter of Sophocles or the blank verse of Shakspere, but roughly corresponds to the Greek choruses or the occasional rhymed songs of the Elizabethan stage. In other words, the verse portion of a Sanskrit drama is not narrative; it is sometimes descriptive, but more commonly lyrical: each stanza sums up the emotional impression which the preceding action or dialogue has made upon one of the actors. Such matter is in English cast into the form of the rhymed stanza; and so, although rhymed verse is very rarely employed in classical Sanskrit, it seems the most appropriate vehicle for the translation of the stanzas of a Sanskrit drama. It is true that we occasionally find stanzas which might fitly be rendered in English blank verse, and, more frequently, stanzas which are so prosaic as not to deserve a rendering in English verse at all.[1] But, as the present translation may be regarded as in some sort an experiment, I have preferred to hold rigidly to the distinction found in the original between simple prose and types of stanza which seem to me to correspond to English rhymed verse.

It is obvious that a translation into verse, and especially into rhymed verse, cannot be as literal as a translation into prose; this

[1] Stanzas of the latter sort in The Little Clay Cart are vii. 2 and viii. 5.

disadvantage I have used my best pains to minimize. I hope it may be said that nothing of real moment has been omitted from the verses; and where lack of metrical skill has compelled expansion, I have striven to make the additions as insignificant as possible.

There is another point, however, in which it is hardly feasible to imitate the original; this is the difference in the dialects used by the various characters. In The Little Clay Cart, as in other Indian dramas, some of the characters speak Sanskrit, others Prākrit. Now Prākrit is the generic name for a number of dialects derived from the Sanskrit and closely akin to it. The inferior personages of an Indian play, and, with rare exceptions, all the women, speak one or another of these Prākrits. Of the thirty characters of this play, for example, only five (Chārudatta, the courtier, Aryaka, Sharvilaka, and the judge) speak Sanskrit;[1] the others speak various Prākrit dialects. Only in the case of Sansthānaka have I made a rude attempt to suggest the dialect by substituting *sh* for *s* as he does. And the grandiloquence of Sharvilaka's Sanskrit in the satirical portion of the third act I have endeavored to imitate.

Whenever the language of the original is at all technical, the translator labors under peculiar difficulty. Thus the legal terms found in the ninth act are inadequately rendered, and, to some extent at least, inevitably so; for the legal forms, or lack of forms, pictured there were never contemplated by the makers of the English legal vocabulary. It may be added here that in rendering from a literature so artificial as the Sanskrit, one must lose not only the sensuous beauty of the verse, but also many plays on words.

In regard to the not infrequent repetitions found in the text, I

[1] This statement requires a slight limitation; compare, for example, the footnote to page 82.

have used my best judgment. Such repetitions have been given in full where it seemed to me that the force or unity of the passage gained by such treatment, or where the original repeats in full, as in the case of v. 7, which is identical with iii. 29. Elsewhere, I have merely indicated the repetition after the manner of the original.

The reader will notice that there was little effort to attain realism in the presentation of an Indian play. He need not be surprised therefore to find (page 145) that Vīraka leaves the court-room, mounts a horse, rides to the suburbs, makes an investigation and returns—all within the limits of a stage-direction. The simplicity of presentation also makes possible sudden shifts of scene. In the first act, for example, there are six scenes, which take place alternately in Chārudatta's house and in the street outside. In those cases where a character enters "seated" or "asleep," I have substituted the verb "appear" for the verb "enter"; yet I am not sure that this concession to realism is wise.

The system of transliteration which I have adopted is intended to render the pronunciation of proper names as simple as may be to the English reader. The consonants are to be pronounced as in English,[1] the vowels as in Italian. Diacritical marks have been avoided, with the exception of the macron. This sign has been used consistently[2] to mark long vowels except *e* and *o*, which are always long. Three rules suffice for the placing of the accent. A long penult is accented: Maitréya, Chārudátta. If the penult is short, the antepenult is accented provided it be long: Sansthā́naka. If both penult and antepenult of a four-syllabled word are short, the pre-antepenultimate receives the accent: Mádanikā, Sthā́varaka.

[1] But the combination *th* should be pronounced as in *ant-hill*, not as in *thin* or *this;* similarly *dh* as in *mad-house; bh* as in *abhor*.

[2] Except in the names Āryaka and Āhīnta, where typographical considerations have led to the omission of the macron over the initial letter; and except also in head-lines.

## III. AN OUTLINE OF THE PLOT

Act I., entitled *The Gems are left Behind.* Evening of the first day.—After the prologue, Chārudatta, who is within his house, converses with his friend Maitreya, and deplores his poverty. While they are speaking, Vasantasenā appears in the street outside. She is pursued by the courtier and Sansthānaka; the latter makes her degrading offers of his love, which she indignantly rejects. Chārudatta sends Maitreya from the house to offer sacrifice, and through the open door Vasantasenā slips unobserved into the house. Maitreya returns after an altercation with Sansthānaka, and recognizes Vasantasenā. Vasantasenā leaves a casket of gems in the house for safe keeping and returns to her home.

Act II., entitled *The Shampooer who Gambled.* Second day.—The act opens in Vasantasenā's house. Vasantasenā confesses to her maid Madanikā her love for Chārudatta. Then a shampooer appears in the street, pursued by the gambling-master and a gambler, who demand of him ten gold-pieces which he has lost in the gambling-house. At this point Darduraka enters, and engages the gambling-master and the gambler in an angry discussion, during which the shampooer escapes into Vasantasenā's house. When Vasantasenā learns that the shampooer had once served Chārudatta, she pays his debt; the grateful shampooer resolves to turn monk. As he leaves the house he is attacked by a runaway elephant, and saved by Karnapūraka, a servant of Vasantasenā.

Act III., entitled *The Hole in the Wall.* The night following the second day.—Chārudatta and Maitreya return home after midnight from a concert, and go to sleep. Maitreya has in his hand the gem-casket which Vasantasenā has left behind. Sharvilaka enters. He is in love with Madanikā, a maid of Vasantasenā's, and is resolved to acquire by theft the means of buying her freedom. He makes a hole in the wall of the house, enters, and steals the casket of gems which Vasantasenā had left. Chārudatta wakes to find casket and thief gone. His wife gives him her pearl necklace with which to make restitution.

Act IV., entitled *Madanikā and Sharvilaka.* Third day.—Sharvilaka comes to Vasantasenā's house to buy Madanikā's freedom. Vasantasenā overhears the facts concerning the theft of her gem-casket from Chārudatta's house, but accepts the casket, and gives Madanikā her freedom. As Sharvilaka leaves the house, he hears that his friend Aryaka, who had been imprisoned by the king, has escaped and is being pursued. Sharvilaka departs to help him. Maitreya comes from Chārudatta with the pearl necklace, to repay Vasantasenā for the gem-casket. She accepts the necklace also, as giving her an excuse for a visit to Chārudatta.

Act V., entitled *The Storm.* Evening of the third day.—Chārudatta appears in the garden of his house. Here he receives a servant of Vasantasenā, who announces that Vasantasenā is on her way to visit him. Vasantasenā then appears in the street with the courtier; the two describe alternately the violence and beauty of the storm which has suddenly arisen. Vasantasenā dismisses the courtier, enters the garden, and explains to Chārudatta how she has again come into possession of the gem-casket. Meanwhile, the storm has so increased in violence that she is compelled to spend the night at Chārudatta's house.

Act VI., entitled *The Swapping of the Bullock-carts.* Morning of the fourth day.—Here she meets Chārudatta's little son, Rohasena. The boy is peevish because he can now have only a little clay cart to play with, instead of finer toys. Vasantasenā gives him her gems to buy a toy cart of gold. Chārudatta's servant drives up to take Vasantasenā in Chārudatta's bullock-cart to the park, where she is to meet Chārudatta; but while Vasantasenā is making ready, he drives away to get a cushion. Then Sansthānaka's servant drives up with his master's cart, which Vasantasenā enters by mistake. Soon after, Chārudatta's servant returns with his cart. Then the escaped prisoner Aryaka appears and enters Chārudatta's cart. Two policemen come on the scene; they are searching for Aryaka. One of them looks into the cart and discovers Aryaka, but agrees to protect him. This he does by deceiving and finally maltreating his companion.

Act VII., entitled *Aryaka's Escape.* Fourth day.—Chārudatta is awaiting Vasantasenā in the park. His cart, in which Aryaka lies hidden, appears. Chārudatta discovers the fugitive, removes his fetters, lends him the cart, and leaves the park.

Act VIII., entitled *The Strangling of Vasantasenā.* Fourth day.—A Buddhist monk, the shampooer of the second act, enters the park. He has difficulty in escaping from Sansthānaka, who appears with the courtier. Sansthānaka's servant drives in with the cart which Vasantasenā had entered by mistake. She is discovered by Sansthānaka, who pursues her with insulting offers of love. When she repulses him, Sansthānaka gets rid of all witnesses, strangles her, and leaves her for dead. The Buddhist monk enters again, revives Vasantasenā, and conducts her to a monastery.

Act IX., entitled *The Trial.* Fifth day.—Sansthānaka accuses Chārudatta of murdering Vasantasenā for her money. In the course of the trial, it appears that Vasantasenā had spent the night of the storm at Chārudatta's house; that she had left the house the next morning to meet Chārudatta in the park; that there had been a struggle in the park, which apparently ended in the murder of a woman. Chārudatta's friend, Maitreya, enters with the gems which

Vasantasenā had left to buy Chārudatta's son a toy cart of gold. These gems fall to the floor during a scuffle between Maitreya and Sansthānaka. In view of Chārudatta's poverty, this seems to establish the motive for the crime, and Chārudatta is condemned to death.

ACT X., entitled *The End.* Sixth day.—Two headsmen are conducting Chārudatta to the place of execution. Chārudatta takes his last leave of his son and his friend Maitreya. But Sansthānaka's servant escapes from confinement and betrays the truth; yet he is not believed, owing to the cunning displayed by his master. The headsmen are preparing to execute Chārudatta, when Vasantasenā herself appears upon the scene, accompanied by the Buddhist monk. Her appearance puts a summary end to the proceedings. Then news is brought that Aryaka has killed and supplanted the former king, that he wishes to reward Chārudatta, and that he has by royal edict freed Vasantasenā from the necessity of living as a courtezan. Sansthānaka is brought before Chārudatta for sentence, but is pardoned by the man whom he had so grievously injured. The play ends with the usual Epilogue.

## DRAMATIS PERSONAE

CHĀRUDATTA, *a Brahman merchant*
ROHASENA, *his son*
MAITREYA, *his friend*
VARDHAMĀNAKA, *a servant in his house*

SANSTHĀNAKA, *brother-in-law of King* PĀLAKA
STHĀVARAKA, *his servant*
*Another Servant of* SANSTHĀNAKA

*A Courtier*
ARYAKA, *a herdsman who becomes king*
SHARVILAKA, *a Brahman, in love with* MADANIKĀ

*A Shampooer, who becomes a Buddhist monk*
MĀTHURA, *a gambling-master*
DARDURAKA, *a gambler*
*Another Gambler*

KARNAPŪRAKA, KUMBHĪLAKA — *servants of* VASANTASENĀ
VĪRAKA, CHANDANAKA — *policemen*
GOHA, AHĪNTA — *headsmen*
*Bastard pages, in* VASANTASENĀ'S *house*
*A Judge, a Gild-warden, a Clerk, and a Beadle*

VASANTASENĀ, *a courtezan*
*Her Mother*
MADANIKĀ, *maid to* VASANTASENĀ
*Another Maid to* VASANTASENĀ

*The Wife of* CHĀRUDATTA
RADANIKĀ, *a maid in* CHĀRUDATTA'S *house*

### SCENE

UJJAYINĪ (*called also* AVANTI) *and its Environs*

# THE LITTLE CLAY CART

## PROLOGUE

*Benediction upon the audience*

HIS bended knees the knotted girdle holds,
Fashioned by doubling of a serpent's folds;
His sensive organs, so he checks his breath,
Are numbed, till consciousness seems sunk in death;
Within himself, with eye of truth, he sees
The All-soul, free from all activities.
May His, may Shiva's meditation be
Your strong defense; on the Great Self thinks he,
Knowing full well the world's vacuity. 1

And again:

May Shiva's neck shield you from every harm,
That seems a threatening thunder-cloud, whereon,
Bright as the lightning-flash, lies Gaurī's arm. 2

*Stage-director.* Enough of this tedious work, which fritters away the interest of the audience! Let me then most reverently salute the honorable gentlemen, and announce our intention to produce a drama called "The Little Clay Cart." Its author was a man

Who vied with elephants in lordly grace;
Whose eyes were those of the chakora bird
That feeds on moonbeams; glorious his face
As the full moon; his person, all have heard,
Was altogether lovely. First in worth
Among the twice-born was this poet, known
As Shūdraka far over all the earth,—
His virtue's depth unfathomed and alone. 3

And again:

The Sāmaveda, the Rigveda too,
The science mathematical, he knew;
The arts wherein fair courtezans excel,
And all the lore of elephants as well.
Through Shiva's grace, his eye was never dim;
He saw his son a king in place of him.
The difficult horse-sacrifice he tried
Successfully; entered the fiery tide,
One hundred years and ten days old, and died. 4

And yet again:

Eager for battle; sloth's determined foe;
  Of scholars chief, who to the Veda cling;
Rich in the riches that ascetics know;
Glad, gainst the foeman's elephant to show
  His valor;—such was Shūdraka, the king. 5

And in this work of his,

Within the town, Avanti named,
Dwells one called Chārudatta, famed
No less for youth than poverty;
A merchant's son and Brahman, he.

His virtues have the power to move
Vasantasenā's inmost love;
Fair as the springtime's radiancy,
And yet a courtezan is she. 6

So here king Shūdraka the tale imparts
Of love's pure festival in these two hearts,
Of prudent acts, a lawsuit's wrong and hate,
A rascal's nature, and the course of fate. 7

[*He walks about and looks around him.*] Why, this music-room of ours is empty. I wonder where the actors have gone. [*Reflecting.*] Ah, I understand.

Empty his house, to whom no child was born;
Thrice empty his, who lacks true friends and sure;
To fools, the world is empty and forlorn;
But all that is, is empty to the poor. 8

I have finished the concert. And I've been practising so long that the pupils of my eyes are dancing, and I'm so hungry that my eyes are crackling like a lotus-seed, dried up by the fiercest rays of the summer sun. I'll just call my wife and ask whether there is anything for breakfast or not.

Hello! here I am—but no! Both the particular occasion and the general custom demand that I speak Prākrit. [*Speaking in Prākrit.*] Confound it! I've been practising so long and I'm so hungry that my limbs are as weak as dried-up lotus-stalks. Suppose I go home and see whether my good wife has got anything ready or not. [*He walks about and looks around him.*] Here I am at home. I'll just go in. [*He enters and looks about.*] Merciful heavens! Why in the world is everything in our house turned upside down? A long stream of rice-water is flowing down the street. The ground, spotted black where the iron kettle has been rubbed clean, is as lovely as a girl with the beauty-marks of black cosmetic on her face. It smells so good that my hunger seems to blaze up and hurts me more than ever. Has some hidden treasure come to light? or am I hungry enough to think the whole world is made of rice? There surely isn't any breakfast in our house, and I'm starved to death. But everything seems topsyturvy here. One girl is preparing cosmetics, another is weaving garlands of flowers. [*Reflecting.*] What does it all mean? Well, I'll call my good wife and learn the truth. [*He looks toward the dressing-room.*] Mistress, will you come here a moment?

[*Enter an actress.*]

*Actress.* Here I am, sir.

*Director.* You are very welcome, mistress.

*Actress.* Command me, sir. What am I to do?

*Director.* Mistress, I've been practising so long and I'm so hungry that my limbs are as weak as dried-up lotus-stalks. Is there anything to eat in the house or not?

*Actress.* There's everything, sir.

*Director.* Well, what?

*Actress.* For instance—there's rice with sugar, melted butter, curdled milk, rice; and, all together, it makes you a dish fit for heaven. May the gods always be thus gracious to you!

*Director.* All that in our house? or are you joking?

*Actress.* [*Aside.*] Yes, I will have my joke. [*Aloud.*] It's in the market-place, sir.

*Director.* [*Angrily.*] You wretched woman, thus shall your own hope be cut off! And death shall find you out! For my expectations, like a scaffolding, have been raised so high, only to fall again.

*Actress.* Forgive me, sir, forgive me! It was only a joke.

*Director.* But what do these unusual preparations mean? One girl is preparing cosmetics, another is weaving garlands, and the very ground is adorned with sacrificial flowers of five different colors.

*Actress.* This is a fast day, sir.

*Director.* What fast?

*Actress.* The fast for a handsome husband.

*Director.* In this world, mistress, or the next?

*Actress.* In the next world, sir.

*Director.* [*Wrathfully.*] Gentlemen! look at this. She is sacrificing my food to get herself a husband in the next world.

*Actress.* Don't be angry, sir. I am fasting in the hope that you may be my husband in my next birth, too.

*Director.* But who suggested this fast to you?

*Actress.* Your own dear friend Jūrnavriddha.

*Director.* [*Angrily.*] Ah, Jūrnavriddha, son of a slave-wench! When, oh, when shall I see King Pālaka angry with you? Then you will be parted, as surely as the scented hair of some young bride.

*Actress.* Don't be angry, sir. It is only that I may have you in the next world that I celebrate this fast. [*She falls at his feet.*]

*Director.* Stand up, mistress, and tell me who is to officiate at this fast.

*Actress.* Some Brahman of our own sort whom we must invite.

*Director.* You may go then. And I will invite some Brahman of our own sort.

*Actress.* Very well, sir. [*Exit.*

*Director.* [*Walking about.*] Good heavens! In this rich city of Ujjayinī how am I to find a Brahman of our own sort? [*He looks about him.*] Ah, here comes Chārudatta's friend Maitreya. Good! I'll ask him. Maitreya, you must be the first to break bread in our house to-day.

*A voice behind the scenes.* You must invite some other Brahman. I am busy.

*Director.* But, man, the feast is set and you have it all to yourself. Besides, you shall have a present.

*The voice.* I said no once. Why should you keep on urging me?

*Director.* He says no. Well, I must invite some other Brahman. [*Exit.*

END OF THE PROLOGUE

# ACT THE FIRST

## THE GEMS ARE LEFT BEHIND

[*Enter, with a cloak in his hand, Maitreya.*]

*Maitreya.*

YOU must invite some other Brahman. I am busy." And yet I really ought to be seeking invitations from a stranger. Oh, what a wretched state of affairs! When good Chārudatta was still wealthy, I used to eat my fill of the most deliciously fragrant sweetmeats, prepared day and night with the greatest of care. I would sit at the door of the courtyard, where I was surrounded by hundreds of dishes, and there, like a painter with his paint-boxes, I would simply touch them with my fingers and thrust them aside. I would stand chewing my cud like a bull in the city market. And now he is so poor that I have to run here, there, and everywhere, and come home, like the pigeons, only to roost. Now here is this jasmine-scented cloak, which Chārudatta's good friend Jūrnavriddha has sent him. He bade me give it to Chārudatta, as soon as he had finished his devotions. So now I will look for Chārudatta. [*He walks about and looks around him.*] Chārudatta has finished his devotions, and here he comes with an offering for the divinities of the house.

[*Enter Chārudatta as described, and Radanikā.*]

*Chārudatta.* [*Looking up and sighing wearily.*]

Upon my threshold, where the offering
    Was straightway seized by swans and flocking cranes,
The grass grows now, and these poor seeds I fling
    Fall where the mouth of worms their sweetness stains. 9

[*He walks about very slowly and seats himself.*]

*Maitreya.* Chārudatta is here. I must go and speak to him. [*Approaching.*] My greetings to you. May happiness be yours.

*Chārudatta.* Ah, it is my constant friend Maitreya. You are very welcome, my friend. Pray be seated.

*Maitreya.* Thank you. [*He seats himself.*] Well, comrade, here is a jasmine-scented cloak which your good friend Jūrnavriddha has sent. He bade me give it you as soon as you had finished your devotions. [*He presents the cloak. Chārudatta takes it and remains sunk in thought.*] Well, what are you thinking about?

*Chārudatta.* My good friend,

> A candle shining through the deepest dark
> Is happiness that follows sorrow's strife;
> But after bliss when man bears sorrow's mark,
> His body lives a very death-in-life. 10

*Maitreya.* Well, which would you rather, be dead or be poor?

*Chārudatta.* Ah, my friend,

> Far better death than sorrows sure and slow;
> Some passing suffering from death may flow,
> But poverty brings never-ending woe. 11

*Maitreya.* My dear friend, be not thus cast down. Your wealth has been conveyed to them you love, and like the moon, after she has yielded her nectar to the gods, your waning fortunes win an added charm.

*Chārudatta.* Comrade, I do not grieve for my ruined fortunes. But

> This is my sorrow. They whom I
> Would greet as guests, now pass me by.
> "This is a poor man's house," they cry.
> As flitting bees, the season o'er,
> Desert the elephant, whose store
> Of ichor[1] spent, attracts no more. 12

*Maitreya.* Oh, confound the money! It is a trifle not worth thinking about. It is like a cattle-boy in the woods afraid of wasps; it does n't stay anywhere where it is used for food.

[1] During the mating season, a fragrant liquor exudes from the forehead of the elephant. Of this liquor bees are very fond.

*Chārud.* Believe me, friend. My sorrow does not spring
From simple loss of gold;
For fortune is a fickle, changing thing,
Whose favors do not hold;
But he whose sometime wealth has taken wing,
Finds bosom-friends grow cold. 13

Then too:

A poor man is a man ashamed; from shame
Springs want of dignity and worthy fame;
Such want gives rise to insults hard to bear;
Thence comes despondency; and thence, despair;
Despair breeds folly; death is folly's fruit.—
Ah! the lack of money is all evil's root! 14

*Maitreya.* But just remember what a trifle money is, after all, and be more cheerful.

*Chārudatta.* My friend, the poverty of a man is to him
A home of cares, a shame that haunts the mind,
Another form of warfare with mankind;
The abhorrence of his friends, a source of hate
From strangers, and from each once-loving mate;
But if his wife despise him, then 't were meet
In some lone wood to seek a safe retreat.
The flame of sorrow, torturing his soul,
Burns fiercely, yet contrives to leave him whole. 15

Comrade, I have made my offering to the divinities of the house. Do you too go and offer sacrifice to the Divine Mothers at a place where four roads meet.

*Maitreya.* No!

*Chārudatta.* Why not?

*Maitreya.* Because the gods are not gracious to you even when thus honored. So what is the use of worshiping?

*Chārudatta.* Not so, my friend, not so! This is the constant duty of a householder.

The gods feel ever glad content
In the gifts, and the self-chastisement,
The meditations, and the prayers,
Of those who banish worldly cares. 16

Why then do you hesitate? Go and offer sacrifice to the Mothers.

*Maitreya.* No, I'm not going. You must send somebody else. Anyway, everything seems to go wrong with me, poor Brahman that I am! It's like a reflection in a mirror; the right side becomes the left, and the left becomes the right. Besides, at this hour of the evening, people are abroad upon the king's highway—courtezans, courtiers, servants, and royal favorites. They will take me now for fair prey, just as the black-snake out frog-hunting snaps up the mouse in his path. But what will you do sitting here?

*Chārudatta.* Good then, remain; and I will finish my devotions.

*Voices behind the scenes.* Stop, Vasantasenā, stop!

[*Enter Vasantasenā, pursued by the courtier, by Sansthānaka, and the servant.*]

*Courtier.* Vasantasenā! Stop, stop!

Ah, why should fear transform your tenderness?
Why should the dainty feet feel such distress,
That twinkle in the dance so prettily?
Why should your eyes, thus startled into fear,
Dart sidelong looks? Why, like the timid deer
Before pursuing hunters, should you flee? 17

*Sansthānaka.* Shtop,[1] Vasantasenā, shtop!

Why flee? and run? and shtumble in your turning?
Be kind! You shall not die. Oh, shtop your feet!
With love, shweet girl, my tortured heart is burning,
As on a heap of coals a piece of meat. 18

[1] The most striking peculiarity of Sansthānaka's dialect—his substitution of *sh* for *s*—I have tried to imitate in the translation.

*Servant.* Stop, courtezan, stop!

In fear you flee
Away from me,
As a summer peahen should;
But my lord and master
Struts fast and faster,
Like a woodcock in the wood. 19

*Courtier.* Vasantasenā! Stop, stop!

Why should you tremble, should you flee,
A-quiver like the plantain tree?
Your garment's border, red and fair,
Is all a-shiver in the air;
Now and again, a lotus-bud
Falls to the ground, as red as blood.
A red realgar[1] vein you seem,
Whence, smitten, drops of crimson stream. 20

*Sansthānaka.* Shtop, Vasantasenā, shtop!

You wake my passion, my desire, my love;
You drive away my shleep in bed at night;
Both fear and terror sheem your heart to move;
You trip and shtumble in your headlong flight.
But Rāvana forced Kuntī[2] to his will;
Jusht sho shall I enjoy you to the fill. 21

*Courtier.* Ah, Vasantasenā,

Why should your fleeter flight
Outstrip my flying feet?
Why, like a snake in fright
Before the bird-king's might,
Thus seek to flee, my sweet?

[1] Red arsenic, used as a cosmetic.

[2] Here, as elsewhere, Sansthānaka's mythology is wildly confused. To a Hindu the effect must be ludicrous enough; but the humor is necessarily lost in a translation. It therefore seems hardly worth while to explain his mythological vagaries in detail.

Could I not catch the storm-wind in his flight?
Yet would not seize upon you, though I might. 22

*Sansthānaka.* Lishten to me, shir!

Thish whip of robber Love, thish dancing-girl,
Eater of fish, deshtroyer of her kin,
Thish shnubnose, shtubborn, love-box, courtezan,
Thish clothes-line, wanton creature, maid of sin—
I gave her ten shweet names, and shtill
She will not bend her to my will. 23

*Courtier.* As courtier's fingers strike the lute's tense string,
The dancing ear-ring smites your wounded cheek.
Why should you flee, with dreadful terror weak,
As flees the crane when heaven's thunders ring? 24

*Sansth.* Your jingling gems, girl, clink like anything;
Like Draupadī you flee, when Rāma kisshed her.
I'll sheize you quick, as once the monkey-king
Sheized Subhadrā, Vishvāvasu's shweet shishter. 25

*Servant.* He's the royal protégé;
Do whatever he may say,
And you shall have good fish and flesh to eat.
For when dogs have all the fish
And the flesh that they can wish,
Even carrion seems to them no longer sweet. 26

*Courtier.* Mistress Vasantasenā,

The girdle drooping low upon your lips
Flashes as brilliant as the shining stars;
The wondrous terror of your fleeing mars
Your charms; for red realgar, loosened, slips
As on an imaged god, from cheek and lips. 27

*Sansth.* We're chasing you with all our main and might,
As dogs a jackal when they hunt and find it;
But you are quick and nimble in your flight,
And shteal my heart with all the roots that bind it. 28

*Vasantasenā.* Pallavaka! Parabhritikā!

*Sansthānaka.* Mashter! a man! a man!

*Courtier.* Don't be a coward.

*Vasantasenā.* Mādhavikā! Mādhavikā!

*Courtier.* [*Laughing.*] Fool! She is calling her servants.

*Sansthānaka.* Mashter! Is she calling a woman?

*Courtier.* Why, of course.

*Sansthānaka.* Women! I kill hundreds of 'em. I'm a brave man.

*Vasantasenā.* [*Seeing that no one answers.*] Alas, how comes it that my very servants have fallen away from me? I shall have to defend myself by mother-wit.

*Courtier.* Don't stop the search.

*Sansthānaka.* Shqueal, Vasantasenā, shqueal for your cuckoo Parabhritikā, or for your blosshom Pallavaka or for all the month of May! Who's going to save you when I'm chasing you?

> Why shpeak of Bhīmasena? Or the shon
> Of Jamadagni, that thrice-mighty one?
> The ten-necked ogre? Shon of Kuntī fair?
> Jusht look at me! My fingers in your hair,
> Jusht like Duhshāsana, I'll tear, and tear. 29

Look, look!

> My shword is sharp; good-by, poor head!
> Let's chop it off, or kill you dead.
> Then do not try my wrath to shun;
> When you musht die, your life is done. 30

*Vasantasenā.* Sir, I am a weak woman.

*Courtier.* That is why you are still alive.

*Sansthānaka.* That is why you're not murdered.

*Vasantasenā.* [*Aside.*] Oh! his very courtesy frightens me. Come, I will try this. [*Aloud.*] Sir, what do you expect from this pursuit? my jewels?

*Courtier*. Heaven forbid! A garden creeper, mistress Vasantasenā, should not be robbed of its blossoms. Say no more about the jewels.

*Vasantasenā*. What is then your desire?

*Sansthānaka*. I'm a man, a big man, a regular Vāsudeva.[1] You musht love me.

*Vasantasenā*. [*Indignantly*.] Heavens! You weary me. Come, leave me! Your words are an insult.

*Sansthānaka*. [*Laughing and clapping his hands*.] Look, mashter, look! The courtezan's daughter is mighty affectionate with me, isn't she? Here she says "Come on! Heavens, you're weary. You're tired!" No, I have n't been walking to another village or another city. No, little mishtress, I shwear by the gentleman's head, I shwear by my own feet! It's only by chasing about at your heels that I've grown tired and weary.

*Courtier*. [*Aside*.] What! is it possible that the idiot does not understand when she says "You weary me"? [*Aloud*.] Vasantasenā, your words have no place in the dwelling of a courtezan,

Which, as you know, is friend to every youth;
  Remember, you are common as the flower
That grows beside the road; in bitter truth,
  Your body has its price; your beauty's dower
Is his, who pays the market's current rate:
Then serve the man you love, and him you hate. 31

And again:

The wisest Brahman and the meanest fool
Bathe in the selfsame pool;
Beneath the peacock, flowering plants bend low,
No less beneath the crow;
The Brahman, warrior, merchant, sail along
With all the vulgar throng.
You are the pool, the flowering plant, the boat;
And on your beauty every man may dote. 32

[1] A name of Krishna, who is perhaps the most amorous character in Indian story.

*Vasantasenā.* Yet true love would be won by virtue, not violence.

*Sansthānaka.* But, mashter, ever since the shlave-wench went into the park where Kāma's[1] temple shtands, she has been in love with a poor man, with Chārudatta, and she doesn't love me any more. His house is to the left. Look out and don't let her shlip out of our hands.

*Courtier.* [*Aside.*] Poor fool, he has said the very thing he should have concealed. So Vasantasenā is in love with Chārudatta? The proverb is right. Pearl suits with pearl. Well, I have had enough of this fool. [*Aloud.*] Did you say the good merchant's house was to the left, you jackass?

*Sansthānaka.* Yes. His house is to the left.

*Vasantasenā.* [*Aside.*] Oh, wonderful! If his house is really at my left hand, then the scoundrel has helped me in the very act of hurting me, for he has guided me to my love.

*Sansthānaka.* But mashter, it 's pitch dark and it 's like hunting for a grain of soot in a pile of shpotted beans. Now you shee Vasantasenā and now you don't.

*Courtier.* Pitch dark it is indeed.

The sudden darkness seems to steal
  The keenness of my sight;
My open eyes, as with a seal,
  Are closed by blackest night. 33

And again:

Darkness anoints my body, and the sky
Drops ointment of thick darkness, till mine eye
  Is all unprofitable grown to me,
Like service done to them who cheat and lie. 34

*Sansthānaka.* Mashter, I 'm looking for Vasantasenā.

*Courtier.* Is there anything you can trace her by, jackass?

*Sansthānaka.* Like what, for inshtance?

[1] Cupid.

*Courtier.* Like the tinkling of her jewels, for instance, or the fragrance of her garlands.

*Sansthānaka.* I hear the shmell of her garlands, but my nose is shtuffed so full of darkness that I don't shee the shound of her jewels very clearly.

*Courtier.* [*To Vasantasenā. Aside.*] Vasantasenā,

'T is true, the night is dark, O timid maid,
And like the lightning hidden in the cloud,
You are not seen; yet you will be betrayed
By fragrant garlands and by anklets loud. 35

Have you heard me, Vasantasenā?

*Vasantasenā.* [*To herself.*] Heard and understood. [*She removes the ankle-rings, lays aside the garlands, and takes a few steps, feeling her way.*] I can feel the wall of the house, and here is a side-entrance. But alas! my fingers tell me that the door is shut.

*Chārudatta* [*who is within the house*]. Comrade, my prayer is done. Go now and offer sacrifice to the Mothers.

*Maitreya.* No, I'm not going.

*Chārudatta.* Alas!

The poor man's kinsmen do not heed his will;
The friends who loved him once, now stand afar;
His sorrows multiply; his strength is nil;
Behold! his character's bright-shining star
Fades like the waning moon; and deeds of ill
That others do, are counted to him still. 36

And again:

No man holds converse with him; none will greet
With due respect the poor man when they meet.
Where rich men hold a feast, if he draw near,
He meets with scornful looks for looks of cheer.

Where vulgar throngs are gathered, 't is the same;
His scanty raiment wakes his heartfelt shame.
Five are the deadly sins[1] we knew before;
Alas! I find the sixth is—to be poor. 37

And yet again:

Ah, Poverty, I pity thee, that so
To me thou clingest, as thy dearest friend;
When my poor life has met its woeful end,
I sadly wonder, whither thou wilt go. 38

*Maitreya.* [*Betraying his embarrassment.*] Well, comrade, if I must go, at least let Radanikā go with me, to keep me company.

*Chārudatta.* Radanikā, you are to accompany Maitreya.

*Radanikā.* Yes, sir.

*Maitreya.* Mistress Radanikā, do you take the offering and the candle while I open the side-door. [*He does so.*]

*Vasantasenā.* It seems as if the door took pity on me and opened of itself. I will lose no time, but enter. [*She looks in.*] What? a candle? Oh dear, oh dear! [*She puts it out with her skirt and enters.*]

*Chārudatta.* What was that, Maitreya?

*Maitreya.* I opened the side-door and the wind came through all in a lump and blew out the candle. Suppose you go out by the side-door, Radanikā, and I will follow as soon as I have gone into the courtyard and lighted the candle again. [*Exit.*

*Sansthānaka.* Mashter! mashter! I 'm looking for Vasantasenā.

*Courtier.* Keep on looking, keep on looking!

*Sansthānaka.* [*Does so.*] Mashter! mashter! I 've caught her! I 've caught her!

*Courtier.* Idiot, you 've caught me.

*Sansthānaka.* You shtand right here, mashter, and shtay where you 're put. [*He renews the search and seizes the servant.*] Mashter!

[1] The five deadly sins are: the slaying of a Brahman, the drinking of wine, theft, adultery with the wife of one's teacher, and association with one guilty of these crimes.

mashter! I 've caught her! I 've caught her!

*Servant.* Master, you 've caught me, your servant.

*Sansthānaka.* Mashter here, shervant here! Mashter, shervant; shervant, mashter. Now shtay where you 're put, both of you. [*He renews the search and seizes Radanikā by the hair.*] Mashter! mashter! Thish time I 've caught her! I 've caught Vasantasenā!

Through the black night she fled, fled she;
Her garland's shmell betrayed her;
Like Chānakya caught Draupadī,
I caught her hair and shtayed her. 39

*Courtier.* Ah, proud to be so young, so fair!
Too high thy love must not aspire;
For now thy blossom-fragrant hair,
That merits richest gems and rare,
Serves but to drag thee through the mire. 40

*Sansth.* I 've got your head, girl, got it tight,
By the hair, the locks, and the curls, too.
Now shcream, shqueak, shqueal with all your might
"Shiva! Ishvara! Shankara! Shambhu!"[1] 41

*Radanikā.* [*In terror.*] Oh, sirs, what does this mean?

*Courtier.* You jackass! It 's another voice.

*Sansthānaka.* Mashter, the wench has changed her voice, the way a cat changes her voice, when she wants shome cream of curdled milk.

*Courtier.* Changed her voice? Strange! Yet why so strange?
She trod the stage; she learned the arts;
She studied to deceive our hearts;
And now she practises her parts. 42

[*Enter Maitreya.*]

*Maitreya.* Look! In the gentle evening breeze the flame of the candle is fluttering like the heart of a goat that goes to the altar. [*He approaches and discovers Radanikā.*] Mistress Radanikā!

[1] These are all epithets of the same god.

*Sansthānaka.* Mashter, mashter! A man! a man!

*Maitreya.* This is right, this is perfectly right, that strangers should force their way into the house, just because Chārudatta is poor.

*Radanikā.* Oh, Maitreya, see how they insult me.

*Maitreya.* What! insult you? No, they are insulting us.

*Radanikā.* Very well. They are insulting you, then.

*Maitreya.* But they are n't using violence?

*Radanikā.* Yes, yes!

*Maitreya.* Really?

*Radanikā.* Really.

*Maitreya.* [*Raising his staff angrily.*] No, sir! Man, a dog will show his teeth in his own kennel, and I am a Brahman! My staff is crooked as my fortunes, but it can still split a dry bamboo or a rascal's pate.

*Courtier.* Have mercy, O great Brahman, have mercy.

*Maitreya.* [*Discovers the courtier.*] He is not the sinner. [*Discovers Sansthānaka.*] Ah, here is the sinner. Well, you brother-in-law to the king, Sansthānaka, you scoundrel, you coward, this is perfectly proper, is n't it? Chārudatta the good is a poor man now—true, but are not his virtues an ornament to Ujjayinī? And so men break into his house and insult his servants!

Insult not him, laid low by poverty;
  For none are counted poor by mighty fate:
  Yet he who falls from virtue's high estate,
Though he be rich, no man is poor as he. 43

*Courtier.* [*Betraying his embarrassment.*] Have mercy, O great Brahman, have mercy. We intended no insolence; we merely mistook this lady for another. For

We sought an amorous maiden,

*Maitreya.* What! this one?

*Courtier.* Heaven forbid!

one whose youth
  Is in the guidance of her own sweet will;

She disappeared; unconscious of the truth,
We did what seems a purposed deed of ill. 44

I pray you, accept this all-in-all of humblest supplication. [*He drops his sword, folds his hands, and falls at Maitreya's feet.*]

*Maitreya.* Good man, rise, rise. When I reviled you, I did not know you. Now I know you and I ask your pardon.

*Courtier.* It is I who should ask pardon. I will rise on one condition.

*Maitreya.* And that is—

*Courtier.* That you will not tell Chārudatta what has happened here.

*Maitreya.* I will be silent.

*Courtier.* Brahman, this gracious act of thine
I bow my neck to bear;
For never could this sword of mine
With virtue's steel compare. 45

*Sansthānaka.* [*Indignantly.*] But mashter, what makes you fold your hands sho helplesshly and fall at the feet of thish manikin?

*Courtier.* I was afraid.

*Sansthānaka.* What were *you* afraid of?

*Courtier.* Of Chārudatta's virtues.

*Sansthānaka.* Virtues? He? You can go into his houshe and not find a thing to eat.

*Courtier.* No, no.
His loving-kindness unto such as we
Has brought him low at last;
From him could no man learn what insults be,
Or e'er his wealth was past.
This well-filled pool, that in its summer day
Gave others drink, itself is dried away. 46

*Sansthānaka.* [*Impatiently.*] Who is the shon of a shlave-wench anyway?

Brave Shvetaketu is he, Pāndu's child?
Or Rādhā's shon, the ten-necked ogre wild?

Or Indradatta? or again, is he
Shon of brave Rāma and of fair Kuntī?
Or Dharmaputra? Ashvatthāman bold?
Perhaps Jatāyu's shelf, that vulture old? 47

*Courtier*. Fool! I will tell you who Chārudatta is.

A tree of life to them whose sorrows grow,
Beneath its fruit of virtue bending low;
Father to good men; virtue's touchstone he;
The mirror of the learned; and the sea
Where all the tides of character unite;
A righteous man, whom pride could never blight;
A treasure-house, with human virtues stored;
Courtesy's essence, honor's precious hoard.
He doth to life its fullest meaning give,
So good is he; we others breathe, not live. 48

Let us be gone.

*Sansthānaka*. Without Vasantasenā?

*Courtier*. Vasantasenā has disappeared.

*Sansthānaka*. How?

*Courtier*. Like sick men's strength, or like the blind man's sight,
Like the fool's judgment, like the sluggard's might,
Like thoughtless scoundrels' store of wisdom's light,
Like love, when foemen fan our slumbering wrath,
So did *she* vanish, when you crossed her path. 49

*Sansthānaka*. I 'm not going without Vasantasenā.

*Courtier*. And did you never hear this?

To hold a horse, you need a rein;
To hold an elephant, a chain;
To hold a woman, use a heart;
And if you have n't one, depart. 50

*Sansthānaka*. If you 're going, go along. I'm not going.

*Courtier*. Very well. I will go. [*Exit*.

*Sansthānaka.* Mashter's gone, sure enough. [*To Maitreya.*] Well, you man with the head that looks like a caret, you manikin, take a sheat, take a sheat.

*Maitreya.* We have already been invited to take a seat.

*Sansthānaka.* By whom?

*Maitreya.* By destiny.

*Sansthānaka.* Shtand up, then, shtand up!

*Maitreya.* We shall.

*Sansthānaka.* When?

*Maitreya.* When fate is kind again.

*Sansthānaka.* Weep, then, weep!

*Maitreya.* We have wept.

*Sansthānaka.* Who made you?

*Maitreya.* Poverty.

*Sansthānaka.* Laugh, then, laugh!

*Maitreya.* Laugh we shall.

*Sansthānaka.* When?

*Maitreya.* When Chārudatta is happy once more.

*Sansthānaka.* You manikin, give poor little Chārudatta thish meshage from me. "Thish wench with golden ornaments and golden jewels, thish female shtage-manager looking after the rehearsal of a new play, thish Vasantasenā—she has been in love with you ever shince she went into the park where Kāma's temple shtands. And when we tried to conciliate her by force, she went into your houshe. Now if you shend her away yourshelf and hand her over to me, if you reshtore her at once, without any lawshuit in court, then I'll be friends with you forever. But if you don't reshtore her, there will be a fight to the death." Remember:

Shmear a pumpkin-shtalk with cow-dung;
Keep your vegetables dried;
Cook your rice in winter evenings;

And be sure your meat is fried.
Then let 'em shtand, and they will not
Bothershomely shmell and rot. 51

Tell it to him prettily, tell it to him craftily. Tell it to him sho that I can hear it as I roosht in the dove-cote on the top of my own palace. If you shay it different, I 'll chew your head like an apple caught in the crack of a door.

*Maitreya.* Very well. I shall tell him.

*Sansthānaka.* [*Aside.*] Tell me, shervant. Is mashter really gone?

*Servant.* Yes, sir.

*Sansthānaka.* Then we will go as quickly as we can.

*Servant.* Then take your sword, master.

*Sansthānaka.* You can keep it.

*Servant.* Here it is, master. Take your sword, master.

*Sansthānaka.* [*Taking it by the wrong end.*]

My shword, red as a radish shkin,
Ne'er finds the time to molder;
Shee how it shleeps its sheath within!
I put it on my shoulder.
While curs and bitches yelp at me, I roam,
Like a hunted jackal, home. 52

[*Sansthānaka and the servant walk about, then exeunt.*

*Maitreya.* Mistress Radanikā, you must not tell good Chārudatta of this outrage. I am sure you would only add to the poor man's sorrows.

*Radanikā.* Good Maitreya, you know Radanikā. Her lips are sealed.

*Maitreya.* So be it.

*Chārudatta.* [*To Vasantasenā.*] Radanikā, Rohasena likes the fresh air, but he will be cold in the evening chill. Pray bring him into the house, and cover him with this mantle. [*He gives her the mantle.*]

*Vasantasenā.* [*To herself.*] See! He thinks I am his servant. [*She takes the mantle and perceives its perfume. Ardently to herself.*] Oh, beautiful! The mantle is fragrant with jasmine. His youthful days are not wholly indifferent to the pleasures of the world. [*She wraps it about her, without letting Chārudatta see.*]

*Chārudatta.* Come, Radanikā, take Rohasena and enter the heart of the house.

*Vasantasenā.* [*To herself.*] Ah me unhappy, that have little part or lot in your heart!

*Chārudatta.* Come, Radanikā, will you not even answer? Alas!

> When man once sees that miserable day,
> When fate almighty sweeps his wealth away,
> Then ancient friendships will no longer hold,
> Then all his former bosom-friends grow cold. 53

*Maitreya.* [*Drawing near to Radanikā.*] Sir, here is Radanikā.

*Chārudatta.* Here is Radanikā? Who then is this—

> This unknown lady, by my robe
> Thus clinging, desecrated,

*Vasantasenā.* [*To herself.*] Say rather "consecrated."

*Chārudatta.*

> Until she seems the crescent moon,
> With clouds of autumn[1] mated? 54

But no! I may not gaze upon another's wife.

*Maitreya.* Oh, you need not fear that you are looking at another man's wife. This is Vasantasenā, who has been in love with you ever since she saw you in the garden where Kāma's temple stands.

*Chārudatta.* What! this is Vasantasenā? [*Aside.*]

> My love for whom—my fortune spent—
> My wretched self in twain has rent,
> Like coward's anger, inward bent. 55

[1] Which look pretty, but do not rain. He doubtless means to suggest that the cloak, belonging to a strange man, is as useless to Vasantasenā as the veil of autumn clouds to the earth.

*Maitreya.* My friend, that brother-in-law of the king says—

*Chārudatta.* Well?

*Maitreya.* "This wench with golden ornaments and golden jewels, this female stage-manager looking after the rehearsal of a new play, this Vasantasenā—she has been in love with you ever since she went into the park where Kāma's temple stands. And when we tried to conciliate her by force, she went into your house."

*Vasantasenā.* [*To herself.*] "Tried to conciliate me by force"—truly, I am honored by these words.

*Maitreya.* "Now if you send her away yourself and hand her over to me, if you restore her at once, without any lawsuit in court, then I'll be friends with you forever. Otherwise, there will be a fight to the death."

*Chārudatta.* [*Contemptuously.*] He is a fool. [*To himself.*] How is this maiden worthy of the worship that we pay a goddess! For now

> Although I bade her enter, yet she seeks
> To spare my poverty, nor enters here;
> Though men are known to her, yet all she speaks
> Contains no word to wound a modest ear. 56

[*Aloud.*] Mistress Vasantasenā, I have unwittingly made myself guilty of an offense; for I greeted as a servant one whom I did not recognize. I bend my neck to ask your pardon.

*Vasantasenā.* It is I who have offended by this unseemly intrusion. I bow my head to seek your forgiveness.

*Maitreya.* Yes, with your pretty bows you two have knocked your heads together, till they look like a couple of rice-fields. I also bow my head like a camel colt's knee and beseech you both to stand up. [*He does so, then rises.*]

*Chārudatta.* Very well, let us no longer trouble ourselves with conventions.

*Vasantasenā.* [*To herself.*] What a delightfully clever hint! But it would hardly be proper to spend the night, considering how I came hither. Well, I will at least say this much. [*Aloud.*] If I am to receive thus much of your favor, sir, I should be glad to leave these jewels in your house. It was for the sake of the jewels that those scoundrels pursued me.

*Chārudatta.* This house is not worthy of the trust.

*Vasantasenā.* You mistake, sir! It is to men that treasures are entrusted, not to houses.

*Chārudatta.* Maitreya, will you receive the jewels?

*Vasantasenā.* I am much indebted to you. [*She hands him the jewels.*]

*Maitreya.* [*Receiving them.*] Heaven bless you, madam.

*Chārudatta.* Fool! They are only entrusted to us.

*Maitreya.* [*Aside.*] Then the thieves may take them, for all I care.

*Chārudatta.* In a very short time—

*Maitreya.* What she has entrusted to us, belongs to us.

*Chārudatta.* I shall restore them.

*Vasantasenā.* I should be grateful, sir, if this gentleman would accompany me home.

*Chārudatta.* Maitreya, pray accompany our guest.

*Maitreya.* She walks as gracefully as a female swan, and you are the gay flamingo to accompany her. But I am only a poor Brahman, and wherever I go, the people will fall upon me just as dogs will snap at a victim dragged to the cross-roads.

*Chārudatta.* Very well. I will accompany her myself. Let the torches be lighted, to ensure our safety on the highway.

*Maitreya.* Vardhamānaka, light the torches.

*Vardhamānaka.* [*Aside to Maitreya.*] What! light torches without oil?

*Maitreya.* [*Aside to Chārudatta.*] These torches of ours are like courtezans who despise their poor lovers. They won't light up unless you feed them.

*Chārudatta.* Enough, Maitreya! We need no torches. See, we have a lamp upon the king's highway.

Attended by her starry servants all,
And pale to see as a loving maiden's cheeks,
Rises before our eyes the moon's bright ball,
Whose pure beams on the high-piled darkness fall
Like streaming milk that dried-up marshes seeks. 57

[*His voice betraying his passion.*] Mistress Vasantasenā, we have reached your home. Pray enter. [*Vasantasenā gazes ardently at him, then exit.*] Comrade, Vasantasenā is gone. Come, let us go home.

All creatures from the highway take their flight;
The watchmen pace their rounds before our sight;
To forestall treachery, is just and right,
For many sins find shelter in the night. 58

[*He walks about.*] And you shall guard this golden casket by night, and Vardhamānaka by day.

*Maitreya.* Very well. [*Exeunt ambo.*

## ACT THE SECOND

### THE SHAMPOOER[1] WHO GAMBLED

[*Enter a maid.*]

*Maid.*

I AM sent with a message to my mistress by her mother. I must go in and find my mistress. [*She walks about and looks around her.*] There is my mistress. She is painting a picture, and putting her whole heart into it. I must go and speak to her.

[*Then appear the love-lorn Vasantasenā, seated, and Madanikā.*]

*Vasantasenā.* Well, girl, and then—

*Madanikā.* But mistress, you were not speaking of anything. What do you mean?

*Vasantasenā.* Why, what did I say?

*Madanikā.* You said, "and then"—

*Vasantasenā.* [*Puckering her brows.*] Oh, yes. So I did.

*Maid.* [*Approaching.*] Mistress, your mother sends word that you should bathe and then offer worship to the gods.

*Vasantasenā.* You may tell my mother that I shall not take the ceremonial bath to-day. A Brahman must offer worship in my place.

*Maid.* Yes, mistress. [*Exit.*

*Madanikā.* My dear mistress, it is love, not naughtiness, that asks the question—but what does this mean?

*Vasantasenā.* Tell me, Madanikā. How do I seem to you?

*Madanikā.* My mistress is so absent-minded that I know her heart is filled with longing for somebody.

*Vasantasenā.* Well guessed. My Madanikā is quick to fathom another's heart.

*Madanikā.* I am very, very glad. Yes, Kāma is indeed mighty, and

[1] Perhaps *masseur* would be more accurate.

his great festival is welcome when one is young. But tell me, mistress, is it a king, or a king's favorite, whom you worship?

*Vasantasenā.* Girl, I wish to love, not to worship.

*Madanikā.* Is it a Brahman that excites your passion, some youth distinguished for very particular learning?

*Vasantasenā.* A Brahman I should have to reverence.

*Madanikā.* Or is it some young merchant, grown enormously wealthy from visiting many cities?

*Vasantasenā.* A merchant, girl, must go to other countries and leave you behind, no matter how much you love him. And the separation makes you very sad.

*Madanikā.* It is n't a king, nor a favorite, nor a Brahman, nor a merchant. Who is it then that the princess loves?

*Vasantasenā.* Girl! Girl! You went with me to the park where Kāma's temple stands?

*Madanikā.* Yes, mistress.

*Vasantasenā.* And yet you ask, as if you were a perfect stranger.

*Madanikā.* Now I know. Is it the man who comforted you when you asked to be protected?

*Vasantasenā.* Well, what was his name?

*Madanikā.* Why, he lives in the merchants' quarter.

*Vasantasenā.* But I asked you for his name.

*Madanikā.* His name, mistress, is a good omen in itself. His name is Chārudatta.

*Vasantasenā.* [*Joyfully.*] Good, Madanikā, good. You have guessed it.

*Madanikā.* [*Aside.*] So much for that. [*Aloud.*] Mistress, they say he is poor.

*Vasantasenā.* That is the very reason why I love him. For a courtezan who sets her heart on a poor man is blameless in the eyes of the world.

*Madanikā.* But mistress, do the butterflies visit the mango-tree when its blossoms have fallen?

*Vasantasenā.* That is just why we call *that* sort of a girl a butterfly.

*Madanikā.* Well, mistress, if you love him, why don't you go and visit him at once?

*Vasantasenā.* Girl, if I should visit him at once, then, because he can't make any return—no, I don't mean that, but it would be hard to see him.

*Madanikā.* Is that the reason why you left your jewels with him?

*Vasantasenā.* You have guessed it.

*A voice*[1] *behind the scenes.* Oh, sir, a shampooer owes me ten gold-pieces, and he got away from us. Hold him, hold him! [*To the fleeing shampooer.*] Stop, stop! I see you from here. [*Enter hurriedly a frightened shampooer.*]

*Shampooer.* Oh, confound this gambling business!

Freed from its tether, the ace—
  I might better say "ass"—how it kicks me!
And the cast of the dice called the "spear"
  Proves true to its name; for it sticks me. 1

The keeper's whole attention
  Was busy with the score;
So it took no great invention
  To vanish through the door.
But I cannot stand forever
  In the unprotected street.
Is there no one to deliver?
  I would fall before his feet. 2

While the keeper and the gambler are looking somewhere else for me, I'll just walk backwards into this empty temple and turn goddess. [*He makes all sorts of gestures, takes his place, and waits. Enter Māthura and the gambler.*]

[1] That of Māthura, the keeper of the gambling-house.

*Māthura.* Oh, sir, a shampooer owes me ten gold-pieces, and he got away from us. Hold him, hold him! Stop, stop! I see you from here.

*Gambler.* You may run to hell, if they'll take you in;
With Indra, the god, you may stay:
For there's never a god can save your skin,
While Māthura wants his pay. 3

*Māthura.* Oh, whither flee you, nimble rambler,
You that cheat an honest gambler?
You that shake with fear and shiver,
All a-tremble, all a-quiver;
You that cannot trip enough,
On the level ground and rough;
You that stain your social station,
Family, and reputation! 4

*Gambler.* [*Examining the footprints.*] Here he goes. And here the tracks are lost.

*Māthura.* [*Gazes at the footprints. Reflectively.*] Look! The feet are turned around. And the temple has n't any image. [*After a moment's thought.*] That rogue of a shampooer has gone into the temple with his feet turned around.

*Gambler.* Let's follow him.

*Māthura.* All right. [*They enter the temple and take a good look, then make signs to each other.*]

*Gambler.* What! a wooden image?

*Māthura.* Of course not. It's stone. [*He shakes it with all his might, then makes signs.*] What do we care? Come, let's have a game. [*He starts to gamble as hard as he can.*]

*Shampooer.* [*Trying with all his might to repress the gambling fever. Aside.*] Oh, oh!

Oh, the rattle of dice is a charming thing,
When you have n't a copper left;

It works like a drum on the heart of a king,
Of all his realm bereft. 5
For gamblers leap down a mountain steep—
I know I shall not play.
Yet the rattle of dice is as sweet as the peep
Of nightingales in May. 6

*Gambler*. My turn, my turn!

*Māthura*. Not much! it's my turn.

*Shampooer*. [*Coming up quickly from behind.*] Is n't it *my* turn?

*Gambler*. We 've got our man.

*Māthura*. [*Seizing him.*] You jail-bird, you 're caught. Pay me my ten gold-pieces.

*Shampooer*. I 'll pay you this very day.

*Māthura*. Pay me this very minute!

*Shampooer*. I 'll pay you. Only have mercy!

*Māthura*. Come, will you pay me now?

*Shampooer*. My head is getting dizzy. [*He falls to the ground. The others beat him with all their might.*]

*Māthura*. There [*drawing the gamblers' ring*] you're bound by the gamblers' ring.

*Shampooer*. [*Rises. Despairingly.*] What! bound by the gamblers' ring? Confound it! That is a limit which we gamblers can't pass. Where can I get the money to pay him?

*Māthura*. Well then, you must give surety.

*Shampooer*. I have an idea. [*He nudges the gambler.*] I'll give you half, if you'll forgive me the other half.

*Gambler*. All right.

*Shampooer*. [*To Māthura.*] I 'll give you surety for a half. You might forgive me the other half.

*Māthura*. All right. Where 's the harm?

*Shampooer*. [*Aloud.*] You forgave me a half, sir?

*Māthura.* Yes.

*Shampooer.* [*To the gambler.*] And you forgave me a half?

*Gambler.* Yes.

*Shampooer.* Then I think I 'll be going.

*Māthura.* Pay me my ten gold-pieces! Where are you going?

*Shampooer.* Look at this, gentlemen, look at this! Here I just gave surety to one of them for a half, and the other forgave me a half. And even after that he is dunning me, poor helpless me!

*Māthura.* [*Seizing him.*] My name is Māthura, the clever swindler, and you 're not going to swindle me this time. Pay up, jail-bird, every bit of my money, and this minute, too.

*Shampooer.* How can I pay?

*Māthura.* Sell your father and pay.

*Shampooer.* Where can I get a father?

*Māthura.* Sell your mother and pay.

*Shampooer.* Where can I get a mother?

*Māthura.* Sell yourself and pay.

*Shampooer.* Have mercy! Lead me to the king's highway.

*Māthura.* Go ahead.

*Shampooer.* If it must be. [*He walks about.*] Gentlemen, will you buy me for ten gold-pieces from this gambling-master? [*He sees a passer-by and calls out.*] What is that? You wish to know what I can do? I will be your house-servant. What! he has gone without even answering. Well, here 's another. I 'll speak to him. [*He repeats his offer.*] What! this one too takes no notice of me. He is gone. Confound it! I 've had hard luck ever since Chārudatta lost his fortune.

*Māthura.* Will you pay?

*Shampooer.* How can I pay? [*He falls down. Māthura drags him about.*] Good gentlemen, save me, save me! [*Enter Darduraka.*]

*Darduraka.* Yes, gambling is a kingdom without a throne.

You do not mind defeat at all;
Great are the sums you spend and win;
While kingly revenues roll in,
Rich men, like slaves, before you fall. 7

And again:

You earn your coin by gambling,
Your friends and wife by gambling,
Your gifts and food by gambling;
Your last cent goes by gambling. 8

And again:

My cash was taken by the trey;
The deuce then took my health away;
The ace then set me on the street;
The four completed my defeat. 9

[*He looks before him.*] Here comes Māthura, our sometime gambling-master. Well, as I can't escape, I think I'll put on my veil. [*He makes any number of gestures with his cloak, then examines it.*]

This cloth is sadly indigent in thread;
This lovely cloth lets in a lot of light;
This cloth's protective power is nearly fled;
This cloth is pretty when it's rolled up tight. 10

Yet after all, what more could a poor saint do? For you see,

One foot I've planted in the sky,
The other on the ground must lie.[1]
The elevation's rather high,
But the sun stands it. Why can't I? 11

*Māthura.* Pay, pay!

*Shampooer.* How can I pay? [*Māthura drags him about.*]

*Darduraka.* Well, well, what is this I see? [*He addresses a bystander.*] What did you say, sir? "This shampooer is being maltreated by the gambling-master, and no one will save him"? I'll save him myself. [*He presses forward.*] Stand back, stand back!

[1] A humorously exaggerated reference to Indian ascetic practices.

[*He takes a look.*] Well, if this is n't that swindler Māthura. And here is the poor saintly shampooer; a saint to be sure,

> Who does not hang with bended head
>   Rigid till set of sun,
> Who does not rub his back with sand
>   Till boils begin to run,
> Whose shins dogs may not browse upon,
>   As they pass him in their rambling.[1]
> Why should this tall and dainty man
>   Be so in love with gambling? 12

Well, I must pacify Māthura. [*He approaches.*] How do you do, Māthura? [*Māthura returns the greeting.*]

*Darduraka.* What does this mean?

*Māthura.* He owes me ten gold-pieces.

*Darduraka.* A mere bagatelle!

*Māthura.* [*Pulling the rolled-up cloak from under Darduraka's arm.*] Look, gentlemen, look! The man in the ragged cloak calls ten gold-pieces a mere bagatelle.

*Darduraka.* My good fool, don't I risk ten gold-pieces on a cast of the dice? Suppose a man has money—is that any reason why he should put it in his bosom and show it? But you,

> You'll lose your caste, you'll lose your soul,
> For ten gold-pieces that he stole,
> To kill a man that's sound and whole,
>   With five good senses in him. 13

*Māthura.* Ten gold-pieces may be a mere bagatelle to you, sir. To me they are a fortune.

*Darduraka.* Well then, listen to me. Just give him ten more, and let him go to gambling again.

*Māthura.* And what then?

*Darduraka.* If he wins, he will pay you.

[1] See note on page 33.

*Māthura.* And if he does n't win?

*Darduraka.* Then he won't pay you.

*Māthura.* This is no time for nonsense. If you say that, you can give him the money yourself. My name is Māthura. I'm a swindler and I play a crooked game, and I'm not afraid of anybody. You are an immoral scoundrel.

*Darduraka.* Who did you say was immoral?

*Māthura.* You're immoral.

*Darduraka.* Your father is immoral. [*He gives the shampooer a sign to escape.*]

*Māthura.* You cur! That is just the way that you gamble.

*Darduraka.* That is the way I gamble?

*Māthura.* Come, shampooer, pay me my ten gold-pieces.

*Shampooer.* I'll pay you this very day. I'll pay at once. [*Māthura drags him about.*]

*Darduraka.* Fool! You may maltreat him when I am away, but not before my eyes.

[*Māthura seizes the shampooer and hits him on the nose. The shampooer bleeds, faints, and falls flat. Darduraka approaches and interferes. Māthura strikes Darduraka, and Darduraka strikes back.*]

*Māthura.* Oh, oh, you accursèd hound! But I'll pay you for this.

*Darduraka.* My good fool, I was walking peaceably along the street, and you struck me. If you strike me to-morrow in court, then you will open your eyes.

*Māthura.* Yes, I'll open my eyes.

*Darduraka.* How will you open your eyes?

*Māthura.* [*Opening his eyes wide.*] This is the way I'll open my eyes.

[*Darduraka throws dust in Māthura's eyes, and gives the shampooer a sign to escape. Māthura shuts his eyes and falls down. The shampooer escapes.*]

*Darduraka.* [*Aside.*] I have made an enemy of the influential gambling-master Māthura. I had better not stay here. Besides, my good friend Sharvilaka told me that a young herdsman named Aryaka has been designated by a soothsayer as our future king. Now everybody in my condition is running after him. I think I will join myself to him. [*Exit.*

*Shampooer.* [*Trembles as he walks away and looks about him.*] Here is a house where somebody has left the side-door open. I will go in. [*He enters and perceives Vasantasenā.*] Madam, I throw myself upon your protection.

*Vasantasenā.* He who throws himself upon my protection shall be safe. Close the door, girl. [*The maid does so.*]

*Vasantasenā.* What do you fear?

*Shampooer.* A creditor, madam.

*Vasantasenā.* You may open the door now, girl.

*Shampooer.* [*To himself.*] Ah! Her reasons for not fearing a creditor are in proportion to her innocence. The proverb is right:

> The man who knows his strength and bears a load
> Proportioned to that strength, not more nor less,
> Is safe from stumbling and from sore distress,
> Although he wander on a dreary road. 14

That means me.

*Māthura.* [*Wiping his eyes. To the gambler.*] Pay, pay!

*Gambler.* While we were quarreling with Darduraka, sir, the man escaped.

*Māthura.* I broke that shampooer's nose for him with my fist. Come on! Let 's trace him by the blood. [*They do so.*]

*Gambler.* He went into Vasantasenā's house, sir.

*Māthura.* Then that is the end of the gold-pieces.

*Gambler.* Let 's go to court and lodge a complaint.

*Māthura.* The swindler would leave the house and escape. No, we must besiege him and so capture him.

[*Vasantasenā gives Madanikā a sign.*]

*Madanikā.* Whence are you, sir? or who are you, sir? or whose son are you, sir? or what is your business, sir? or what are you afraid of?

*Shampooer.* Listen, madam. My birthplace is Pātaliputra, madam. I am the son of a householder. I practise the trade of a shampooer.

*Vasantasenā.* It is a very dainty art, sir, which you have mastered.

*Shampooer.* Madam, as an art I mastered it. It has now become a mere trade.

*Madanikā.* Your answers are most disconsolate, sir. Pray continue.

*Shampooer.* Yes, madam. When I was at home, I used to hear travelers tell tales, and I wanted to see new countries, and so I came here. And when I had come here to Ujjayinī, I became the servant of a noble gentleman. Such a handsome, courteous gentleman! When he gave money away, he did not boast; when he was injured, he forgot it. To cut a long story short: he was so courteous that he regarded his own person as the possession of others, and had compassion on all who sought his protection.

*Madanikā.* Who may it be that adorns Ujjayinī with the virtues which he has stolen from the object of my mistress' desires?

*Vasantasenā.* Good, girl, good! I had the same thought in mind.

*Madanikā.* But to continue, sir—

*Shampooer.* Madam, he was so compassionate and so generous that now—

*Vasantasenā.* His riches have vanished?

*Shampooer.* I did n't say it. How did you guess it, madam?

*Vasantasenā.* What was there to guess? Virtue and money seldom keep company. In the pools from which men cannot drink there is so much the more water.

*Madanikā.* But sir, what is his name?

*Shampooer*. Madam, who does not know the name of this moon of the whole world? He lives in the merchants' quarter. He whose name is worthy of all honor is named Chārudatta.

*Vasantasenā*. [*Joyfully rising from her seat.*] Sir, this house is your own. Give him a seat, girl, and take this fan. The gentleman is weary. [*Madanikā does as she is bid.*]

*Shampooer*. [*Aside.*] What! so much honor because I mentioned Chārudatta's name? Heaven bless you, Chārudatta! You are the only man in the world who really lives. All others merely breathe. [*He falls at Vasantasenā's feet.*] Enough, madam, enough. Pray be seated, madam.

*Vasantasenā*. [*Seating herself.*] Where is he who is so richly your creditor, sir?

*Shamp*. The good man's wealth consists in kindly deeds;
All other wealth is vain and quickly flies.
The man who honors not his neighbor's needs,
Does that man know what honor signifies? 15

*Vasantasenā*. But to continue—

*Shampooer*. So I became a servant in his employ. And when his wealth was reduced to his virtue, I began to live by gambling. But fate was cruel, and I lost ten gold-pieces.

*Māthura*. I am ruined! I am robbed!

*Shampooer*. There are the gambling-master and the gambler, looking for me. You have heard my story, madam. The rest is your affair.

*Vasantasenā*. Madanikā, the birds fly everywhither when the tree is shaken in which they have their nests. Go, girl, and give the gambling-master and the gambler this bracelet. And tell them that this gentleman sends it. [*She removes a bracelet from her arm, and gives it to Madanikā.*]

*Madanikā*. [*Receiving the bracelet.*] Yes, mistress. [*She goes out.*]

*Māthura.* I am ruined! I am robbed!

*Madanikā.* Inasmuch as these two are looking up to heaven, and sighing, and chattering, and fastening their eyes on the door, I conclude that they must be the gambling-master and the gambler. [*Approaching.*] I salute you, sir.

*Māthura.* May happiness be yours.

*Madanikā.* Sir, which of you is the gambling-master?

*Māth.* O maiden, fair but something less than shy,
With red lip wounded in love's ardent play,
On whom is bent that sweet, coquettish eye?
For whom that lisp that steals the heart away? 16

*I* have n't got any money. You'll have to look somewhere else.

*Madanikā.* You are certainly no gambler, if you talk that way. Is there any one who *owes* you money?

*Māthura.* There is. He owes ten gold-pieces. What of him?

*Madanikā.* In his behalf my mistress sends you this bracelet. No, no! He sends it himself.

*Māthura.* [*Seizing it joyfully.*] Well, well, you may tell the noble youth that his account is squared. Let him come and seek delight again in gambling. [*Exeunt Māthura and the gambler.*

*Madanikā.* [*Returning to Vasantasenā.*] Mistress, the gambling-master and the gambler have gone away well-pleased.

*Vasantasenā.* Go, sir, and comfort your kinsfolk.

*Shampooer.* Ah, madam, if it may be, these hands would gladly practise their art in your service.

*Vasantasenā.* But sir, he for whose sake you mastered the art, who first received your service, he should have your service still.

*Shampooer.* [*Aside.*] A very pretty way to decline my services. How shall I repay her kindness? [*Aloud.*] Madam, thus dishonored as a gambler, I shall become a Buddhist monk. And so, madam, treasure these words in your memory: "He was a shampooer, a gambler, a Buddhist monk."

*Vasantasenā.* Sir, you must not act too precipitately.

*Shampooer.* Madam, my mind is made up. [*He walks about.*]

I gambled, and in gambling I did fall,
Till every one beheld me with dismay.
Now I shall show my honest face to all,
And walk abroad upon the king's highway. 17

[*Tumultuous cries behind the scenes.*]

*Shampooer.* [*Listening.*] What is this? What is this? [*Addressing some one behind the scenes.*] What did you say? "Post-breaker, Vasantasenā's rogue elephant, is at liberty!" Hurrah! I must go and see the lady's best elephant. No, no! What have I to do with these things? I must hold to my resolution. [*Exit.*

[*Then enter hastily Karnapūraka, highly delighted, wearing a gorgeous mantle.*]

*Karnapūraka.* Where is she? Where is my mistress?

*Madanikā.* Insolent! What can it be that so excites you? You do not see your mistress before your very eyes.

*Karnapūraka.* [*Perceiving Vasantasenā.*] Mistress, my service to you.

*Vasantasenā.* Karnapūraka, your face is beaming. What is it?

*Karnapūraka.* [*Proudly.*] Oh, mistress! You missed it! You didn't see Karnapūraka's heroism to-day!

*Vasantasenā.* What, Karnapūraka, what?

*Karnapūraka.* Listen. Post-breaker, my mistress' rogue elephant, broke the stake he was tied to, killed his keeper, and ran into the street, making a terrible commotion. You should have heard the people shriek,

Take care of the babies, as quick as you can,
And climb up a roof or a tree!

The elephant rogue wants the blood of a man.
Escape! Run away! Can't you see? 18

And:

How they lose their ankle-rings!
Girdles, set with gems and things,
Break away from fastenings!

As they stumble, trip, and blunder,
See the bracelets snap asunder,
Each a tangled, pearly wonder! 19

And that rogue of an elephant dives with his trunk and his feet and his tusks into the city of Ujjayinī, as if it were a lotus-pond in full flower. At last he comes upon a Buddhist monk.[1] And while the man's staff and his water-jar and his begging-bowl fly every which way, he drizzles water over him and gets him between his tusks. The people see him and begin to shriek again, crying "Oh, oh, the monk is killed!"

*Vasantasenā.* [*Anxiously.*] Oh, what carelessness, what carelessness!

*Karnapūraka.* Don't be frightened. Just listen, mistress. Then, with a big piece of the broken chain dangling about him, he picked him up, picked up the monk between his tusks, and just then Karnapūraka saw him, *I* saw him, no, no! the slave who grows fat on my mistress' rice-cakes saw him, stumbled with his left foot over a gambler's score, grabbed up an iron pole out of a shop, and challenged the mad elephant—

*Vasantasenā.* Go on! Go on!

*Karnap.* I hit him—in a fit of passion, too—

He really looked like some great mountain peak.
And from between those tusks of his I drew
The sacred hermit meek. 20

*Vasantasenā.* Splendid, splendid! But go on!

*Karnapūraka.* Then, mistress, all Ujjayinī tipped over to one side,

[1] The shampooer, whose transformation is astonishingly sudden.

like a ship loaded unevenly, and you could hear nothing but "Hurrah, hurrah for Karnapūraka!" Then, mistress, a man touched the places where he ought to have ornaments, and, finding that he had n't any, looked up, heaved a long sigh, and threw this mantle over me.

*Vasantasenā.* Find out, Karnapūraka, whether the mantle is perfumed with jasmine or not.

*Karnapūraka.* Mistress, the elephant perfume is so strong that I can't tell for sure.

*Vasantasenā.* Then look at the name.

*Karnapūraka.* Here is the name. You may read it, mistress. [*He hands her the mantle.*]

*Vasantasenā.* [*Reads.*] Chārudatta. [*She seizes the mantle eagerly and wraps it about her.*]

*Madanikā.* The mantle is very becoming to her, Karnapūraka.

*Karnapūraka.* Oh, yes, the mantle is becoming enough.

*Vasantasenā.* Here is your reward, Karnapūraka. [*She gives him a gem.*]

*Karnapūraka.* [*Taking it and bowing low.*] Now the mantle is most wonderfully becoming.

*Vasantasenā.* Karnapūraka, where is Chārudatta now?

*Karnapūraka.* He started to go home along this very street.

*Vasantasenā.* Come, girl! Let us go to the upper balcony and see Chārudatta. [*Exeunt omnes.*

## ACT THE THIRD

### THE HOLE IN THE WALL

[*Enter Chārudatta's servant, Vardhamānaka.*]

*Vardh.* A MASTER, kindly and benevolent,
His servants love, however poor he be.
The purse-proud, with a will on harshness bent,
Pays service in the coin of cruelty. 1

And again:

A bullock greedy for a feast of corn
You never can prevent;
A wife who wants her lord to wear a horn
You never can prevent;
A man who loves to gamble night and morn
You never can prevent;
And blemishes[1] that with a man are born
You never can prevent. 2

It is some time since Chārudatta went to the concert. It is past midnight, and still he does not come. I think I will go into the outer hall and take a nap. [*He does so.*]

[*Enter Chārudatta and Maitreya.*]

*Chārudatta.* How beautifully Rebhila sang! The lute is indeed a pearl, a pearl not of the ocean.

Gently the anxious lover's heart befriending,
Consoling when true lovers may not meet,
To love-lorn souls the dearest comforts sending,
It adds to sweetest love its more of sweet. 3

*Maitreya.* Well then, let 's go into the house.

*Chārudatta.* But how wonderfully Master Rebhila sang!

[1] This refers to Chārudatta's generosity, which continues after his wealth has vanished.

*Maitreya.* There are just two things that always make me laugh. One is a woman talking Sanskrit, and the other is a man who tries to sing soft and low. Now when a woman talks Sanskrit, she is like a heifer with a new rope through her nose; all you hear is "soo, soo, soo." And when a man tries to sing soft and low, he reminds me of an old priest muttering texts, while the flowers in his chaplet dry up. No, I don't like it!

*Chārudatta.* My friend, Master Rebhila sang most wonderfully this evening. And still you are not satisfied.

The notes of love, peace, sweetness, could I trace,
The note that thrills, the note of passion too,
The note of woman's loveliness and grace—
Ah, my poor words add nothing, nothing new!
But as the notes in sweetest cadence rang,
I thought it was my hidden love who sang. 4

The melody of song, the stricken strings
In undertone that half-unconscious clings,
More clearly sounding when the passions rise,
But ever sweeter as the music dies.
Words that strong passion fain would say again,
Yet checks their second utterance—in vain;
For music sweet as this lives on, until
I walk as hearing sweetest music still. 5

*Maitreya.* But see, my friend! The very dogs are sound asleep in the shops that look out on the market. Let us go home. [*He looks before him.*] Look, look! The blessèd moon seems to give place to darkness, as she descends from her palace in heaven.

*Chārudatta.* True.

The moon gives place to darkness as she dips
Behind the western mountain; and the tips
Of her uplifted horns alone appear,
Like two sharp-pointed tusks uplifted clear,

Where bathes an elephant in waters cool,
Who shows naught else above the jungle pool. 6

*Maitreya.* Well, here is our house. Vardhamānaka, Vardhamānaka, open the door!

*Vardhamānaka.* I hear Maitreya's voice. Chārudatta has returned. I must open the door for him. [*He does so.*] Master, I salute you. Maitreya, I salute you too. The couch is ready. Pray be seated. [*Chārudatta and Maitreya enter and seat themselves.*]

*Maitreya.* Vardhamānaka, call Radanikā to wash our feet.

*Chārudatta.* [*Compassionately.*] She sleeps. Do not wake her.

*Vardhamānaka.* I will bring the water, Maitreya, and you may wash Chārudatta's feet.

*Maitreya.* [*Angrily.*] Look, man. He acts like the son of a slave that he is, for he is bringing water. But he makes me wash your feet, and I am a Brahman.

*Chārudatta.* Good Maitreya, do you bring the water, and Vardhamānaka shall wash my feet.

*Vardhamānaka.* Yes, Maitreya. Do you bring the water. [*Maitreya does so. Vardhamānaka washes Chārudatta's feet, then moves away.*]

*Chārudatta.* Let water be brought for the Brahman's feet.

*Maitreya.* What good does water do my feet? I shall have to roll in the dirt again, like a beaten ass.

*Vardhamānaka.* Maitreya, you are a Brahman.

*Maitreya.* Yes, like a slow-worm among all the other snakes, so am I a Brahman among all the other Brahmans.

*Vardhamānaka.* Maitreya, I will wash your feet after all. [*He does so.*] Maitreya, this golden casket I was to keep by day, you by night. Take it. [*He gives it to Maitreya, then exit.*

*Maitreya.* [*Receiving the casket.*] The thing is here still. Is n't there a single thief in Ujjayinī to steal the wretch that robs me of my sleep? Listen. I am going to take it into the inner court.

*Chārud.* Such lax attention we can ill afford.
If we are trusted by a courtezan,
Then, Brahman, prove yourself an honest man,
And guard it safely, till it be restored. 7

[*He nods, repeating the stanza* "The melody of song, the stricken strings:" *page* 44.]

*Maitreya.* Are you going to sleep?

*Chārudatta.* Yes, so it seems.
For conquering sleep, descending on mine eyes,
First smites the brow with unresisted blow;
Unseen, elusive, like old age, she tries
To gather strength by weakening her foe. 8

*Maitreya.* Then let's go to sleep. [*He does so.*]

[*Enter Sharvilaka.*[1]]

*Sharv.* I made an entrance for my body's round
By force of art and arms, a path to deeds!
I skinned my sides by crawling on the ground,
Like a snake that sloughs the skin no longer sound;
And now I go where my profession leads. 9

[*He gazes at the sky. Joyfully.*] See! The blessèd moon is setting. For well I know,
My trade would fain from watchmen's eyes be shrouded;
Valiant, I force the dwelling of another.
But see, the stars in deepest dark are clouded,
And the night shields me like a careful mother. 10

I made a breach in the orchard wall and entered. And now I must force my way into the inner court as well.
Yes, let men call it vulgar, if they will,
The trade that thrives while sleeps the sleepyhead;
Yes, knavery, not bravery, call it still,
To overreach confiding folk a-bed.

[1] The following scene satirizes the Hindu love of system and classification.

Far better blame and hissing, fairly won,
Than the pay of genuflecting underlings;
This antique path was trod by Drona's son,
Who slew the sleeping, unsuspecting kings. 11

But where shall I make the breach?

Where is the spot which falling drops decayed?
For each betraying sound is deadened there.
No yawning breach should in the walls be made,
So treatises on robbery declare.
Where does the palace crumble? Where the place
That niter-eaten bricks false soundness wear?
Where shall I 'scape the sight of woman's face?
Fulfilment of my wishes waits me there. 12

[*He feels the wall.*] Here is a spot weakened by constant sun and sprinkling and eaten by saltpeter rot. And here is a pile of dirt thrown up by a mouse. Now heaven be praised! My venture prospers. This is the first sign of success for Skanda's[1] sons. Now first of all, how shall I make the breach? The blessèd Bearer of the Golden Lance[2] has prescribed four varieties of breach, thus: if the bricks are baked, pull them out; if they are unbaked, cut them; if they are made of earth, wet them; if they are made of wood, split them. Here we have baked bricks; ergo, pull out the bricks.

Now what shall be the shape I give the breach?
A "lotus," "cistern," "crescent moon," or "sun"?
"Oblong," or "cross," or "bulging pot"? for each
The treatises permit. Which one? which one?
And where shall I display my sovereign skill,
That in the morning men may wonder still? 13

In this wall of baked bricks, the "bulging pot" would be effective. I will make that.

[1] The patron saint of thieves. [2] An epithet of Skanda.

At other walls that I have pierced by night,
And at my less successful ventures too,
The crowd of neighbors gazed by morning light,
Assigning praise or blame, as was my due. 14

Praise to the boon-conferring god, to Skanda of immortal youth! Praise to him, the Bearer of the Golden Lance, the Brahman's god, the pious! Praise to him, the Child of the Sun! Praise to him, the teacher of magic, whose first pupil I am! For he found pleasure in me and gave me magic ointment,

With which so I anointed be,
No watchman's eye my form shall see;
And edgèd sword that falls on me
From cruel wounds shall leave me free. 15

[*He anoints himself.*] Alas, I have forgotten my measuring line. [*Reflecting.*] Aha! This sacred cord[1] shall be my measuring line. Yes, the sacred cord is a great blessing to a Brahman, especially to one like me. For, you see,

With this he measures, ere he pierce a wall,
And picks the lock, when jewels are at stake.
It serves as key to bolted door and hall,
As tourniquet for bite of worm and snake. 16

The measuring is done. I begin my task. [*He does so, then takes a look.*] My breach lacks but a single brick. Alas, I am bitten by a snake. [*He binds his finger with the sacred cord, and manifests the workings of poison.*] I have applied the remedy, and now I am restored. [*He continues his work, then gazes.*] Ah, there burns a candle. See!

Though jealous darkness hems it round,
The golden-yellow candle from its place
Shines through the breach upon the ground,
Like a streak of gold upon the touchstone's face. 17

[1] The sacrificial cord, which passes over the left shoulder and under the right arm, is worn constantly by members of the three upper castes.

[*He returns to his work.*] The breach is finished. Good! I enter. But no, I will not enter yet. I will shove a dummy in. [*He does so.*] Ah, no one is there. Praise be to Skanda! [*He enters and looks about.*] See! Two men asleep. Come, for my own protection I will open the door. But the house is old and the door squeaks. I must look for water. Now where might water be? [*He looks about, finds water, and sprinkles the door. Anxiously.*] I hope it will not fall upon the floor and make a noise. Come, this is the way. [*He puts his back against the door and opens it cautiously.*] Good! So much for that. Now I must discover whether these two are feigning sleep, or whether they are asleep in the fullest meaning of the term. [*He tries to terrify them, and notes the effect.*] Yes, they must be asleep in the fullest meaning of the term. For see!

Their breath first calmly rises, ere it sink;
  Its regularity all fear defies.
  Unmoving in their socket-holes, the eyes
Are tightly closed, and never seem to wink.
The limbs relaxed, at ease the bodies lie,
  I see their feet beyond the bedstead peep,
The lighted candle vexes not the eye;
  It would, if they were only feigning sleep. 18

[*He looks about him.*] What! a drum? And here is a flute. And here, a snare-drum. And here, a lute. And reed-pipes. And yonder, manuscripts. Is this the house of a dancing-master? But no! When I entered, I was convinced that this was a palatial residence. Now then, is this man poor in the fullest meaning of the term, or, from fear of the king or of thieves, does he keep his property buried? Well, my own property is buried, too. But I will scatter the seeds that betray subterranean gold. [*He does so.*] The scattered seeds nowhere swell up. Ah, he is poor in the fullest meaning of the term. Good! I go.

*Maitreya.* [*Talking in his sleep.*] Look, man. I see something like a hole in the wall. I see something like a thief. You had better take this golden casket.

*Sharvilaka.* I wonder if the man has discovered that I have entered, and is showing off his poverty in order to make fun of me. Shall I kill him, or is the poor devil talking in his sleep? [*He takes a look.*] But see! This thing wrapped in a ragged bath-clout, now that I inspect it by the light of my candle, is in truth a jewel-casket. Suppose I take it. But no! It is hardly proper to rob a man of good birth, who is as poor as I am. I go.

*Maitreya.* My friend, by the wishes of cows and Brahmans[1] I conjure you to take this golden casket.

*Sharvilaka.* One may not disregard the sacred wish of a cow and the wish of a Brahman. I will take it. But look! There burns the candle. I keep about me a moth for the express purpose of extinguishing candles. I will let him enter the flame. This is his place and hour. May this moth which I here release, depart to flutter above the flame in varying circles. The breeze from the insect's wings has translated the flame into accursèd darkness. Or shall I not rather curse the darkness brought by me upon my Brahmanic family? For my father was a man who knew the four Vedas, who would not accept a gift; and I, Sharvilaka, his son, and a Brahman, I am committing a crime for the sake of that courtezan girl Madanikā. Now I will grant the Brahman's wish. [*He reaches out for the casket.*]

*Maitreya.* How cold your fingers are, man!

*Sharvilaka.* What carelessness! My fingers are cold from touching water. Well, I will put my hand in my armpit. [*He warms his left hand and takes the casket.*]

*Maitreya.* Have you got it?

*Sharvilaka.* I could not refuse a Brahman's request. I have it.

[1] Sacred creatures.

*Maitreya.* Now I shall sleep as peacefully as a merchant who has sold his wares.

*Sharvilaka.* O great Brahman, sleep a hundred years! Alas that a Brahman family should thus be plunged in darkness for the sake of Madanikā, a courtezan! Or better, I myself am thus plunged in darkness.

A curse on poverty, I say!
'T is stranger to the manly will;
This act that shuns the light of day
I curse indeed, but do it still. 19

Well then, I must go to Vasantasenā's house to buy Madanikā's freedom. [*He walks about and looks around him.*] Ah, I think I hear footsteps. I hope they are not those of policemen. Never mind. I will pretend to be a pillar, and wait. But after all, do policemen exist for me, for Sharvilaka? Why, I am

A cat for crawling, and a deer for flight,
A hawk for rending, and a dog for sight
To judge the strength of men that wake or sleep,
A snake, when 't is advisable to creep,
Illusion's self, to seem a saint or rogue,
Goddess of Speech in understanding brogue;
A light in blackest night, in holes a lizard I can be,
A horse on terra firma, and a ship upon the sea. 20

And again:

Quick as a snake, and steady as a hill;
In flight the prince of birds can show no greater skill;
In searching on the ground I am as keen as any hare,
In strength I am a lion, and a wolf to rend and tear. 21

*Radanikā.* [*Entering.*] Dear me! Vardhamānaka went to sleep in the outer court, and now he is not there. Well, I will call Maitreya. [*She walks about.*]

*Sharvilaka.* [*Prepares to strike down Radanikā, but first takes a look.*] What! a woman? Good! I go. [*Exit.*

*Radanikā.* [*Recoiling in terror.*] Oh, oh, a thief has cut a hole in the wall of our house and is escaping. I must go and wake Maitreya. [*She approaches Maitreya.*] Oh, Maitreya, get up, get up! A thief has cut a hole in the wall of our house and has escaped.

*Maitreya.* [*Rising.*] What do you mean, wench? "A hole in the wall has cut a thief and has escaped"?

*Radanikā.* Poor fool! Stop your joking. Don't you see it?

*Maitreya.* What do you mean, wench? "It looks as if a second door had been thrown open"? Get up, friend Chārudatta, get up! A thief has made a hole in the wall of our house and has escaped.

*Chārudatta.* Yes, yes! A truce to your jests!

*Maitreya.* But it is n't a jest. Look!

*Chārudatta.* Where?

*Maitreya.* Why, here.

*Chārudatta.* [*Gazing.*] What a very remarkable hole!

The bricks are drawn away below, above;
  The top is narrow, but the center wide;
  As if the great house-heart had burst with pride,
Fearing lest the unworthy share its love. 22

To think that science should be expended on a task like this!

*Maitreya.* My friend, this hole must have been made by one of two men; either by a stranger, or else for practice by a student of the science of robbery. For what man here in Ujjayinī does not know how much wealth there is in our house?

*Chārud.* Stranger he must have been who made the breach,
  His customed harvest in my house to reap;
He has not learned that vanished riches teach
  A calm, untroubled sleep.

He saw the sometime greatness of my home
And forced an entrance; for his heart did leap
With short-lived hope; now he must elsewhere roam,
And over broken hopes must sorely weep. 23

Just think of the poor fellow telling his friends: "I entered the house of a merchant's son, and found—nothing."

*Maitreya.* Do you mean to say that you pity the rascally robber? Thinks he—"Here's a great house. Here's the place to carry off a jewel-casket or a gold-casket." [*He remembers the casket. Despondently. Aside.*] Where *is* that golden casket? [*He remembers the events of the night. Aloud.*] Look, man! You are always saying "Maitreya is a fool, Maitreya is no scholar." But I certainly acted wisely in handing over that golden casket to you. If I had n't, the son of a slave would have carried it off.

*Chārudatta.* A truce to your jests!

*Maitreya.* Just because I'm a fool, do you suppose I don't even know the place and time for a jest?

*Chārudatta.* But when did this happen?

*Maitreya.* Why, when I told you that your fingers were cold.

*Chārudatta.* It might have been. [*He searches about. Joyfully.*] My friend, I have something pleasant to tell you.

*Maitreya.* What? Was n't it stolen?

*Chārudatta.* Yes.

*Maitreya.* What is the pleasant news, then?

*Chārudatta.* The fact that he did not go away disappointed.

*Maitreya.* But it was only entrusted to our care.

*Chārudatta.* What! entrusted to our care? [*He swoons.*]

*Maitreya.* Come to yourself, man. Is the fact that a thief stole what was entrusted to you, any reason why you should swoon?

*Chārudatta.* [*Coming to himself.*] Ah, my friend,

Who will believe the truth?
  Suspicion now is sure.
This world will show no ruth
  To the inglorious poor. 24

Alas! If envious fate before
  Has wooed my wealth alone,
Why should she seek my store
  Of virtue as her own? 25

*Maitreya.* I intend to deny the whole thing. Who gave anybody anything? who received anything from anybody? who was a witness?

*Chārudatta.* And shall I tell a falsehood now?

No! I will beg until I earn
  The wherewithal my debt to pay.
Ignoble falsehood I will spurn,
  That steals the character away. 26

*Radanikā.* I will go and tell his good wife. [*She goes out, returning with Chārudatta's wife.*]

*Wife.* [*Anxiously.*] Oh! Is it true that my lord is uninjured, and Maitreya too?

*Radanikā.* It is true, mistress. But the gems which belong to the courtezan have been stolen. [*Chārudatta's wife swoons.*] O my good mistress! Come to yourself!

*Wife.* [*Recovering.*] Girl, how can you say that my lord is uninjured? Better that he were injured in body than in character. For now the people of Ujjayinī will say that my lord committed this crime because of his poverty. [*She looks up and sighs.*] Ah, mighty Fate! The destinies of the poor, uncertain as the water-drops which fall upon a lotus-leaf, seem to thee but playthings. There remains to me this one necklace, which I brought with me from my mother's house. But my lord would be too proud to accept it. Girl, call Maitreya hither.

*Radanikā*. Yes, mistress. [*She approaches Maitreya.*] Maitreya, my lady summons you.

*Maitreya*. Where is she?

*Radanikā*. Here. Come!

*Maitreya*. [*Approaching.*] Heaven bless you!

*Wife*. I salute you, sir. Sir, will you look straight in front of you?

*Maitreya*. Madam, here stands a man who looks straight in front of him.

*Wife*. Sir, you must accept this.

*Maitreya*. Why?

*Wife*. I have observed the Ceremony of the Gems. And on this occasion one must make as great a present as one may to a Brahman. This I have not done, therefore pray accept this necklace.

*Maitreya*. [*Receiving the necklace.*] Heaven bless you! I will go and tell my friend.

*Wife*. You must not do it in such a way as to make me blush, Maitreya. [*Exit.*

*Maitreya*. [*In astonishment.*] What generosity!

*Chārudatta*. How Maitreya lingers! I trust his grief is not leading him to do what he ought not. Maitreya, Maitreya!

*Maitreya*. [*Approaching.*] Here I am. Take that. [*He displays the necklace.*]

*Chārudatta*. What is this?

*Maitreya*. Why, that is the reward you get for marrying such a wife.

*Chārudatta*. What! my wife takes pity on me? Alas, now am I poor indeed!

> When fate so robs him of his all,
> That on her pity he must call,
> The man to woman's state doth fall,
> The woman is the man. 27

But no, I am not poor. For I have a wife

Whose love outlasts my wealthy day;
In thee a friend through good and ill;
And truth that naught could take away:
Ah, this the poor man lacketh still. 28

Maitreya, take the necklace and go to Vasantasenā. Tell her in my name that we have gambled away the golden casket, forgetting that it was not our own; that we trust she will accept this necklace in its place.

*Maitreya.* But you must not give away this necklace, the pride of the four seas, for that cheap thing that was stolen before we had a bite or a drink out of it.

*Chārudatta.* Not so, my friend.

She showed her trust in leaving us her treasure;
The price of confidence has no less measure. 29

Friend, I conjure you by this gesture, not to return until you have delivered it into her hands. Vardhamānaka, do you speedily

Fill up the opening with the selfsame bricks;
Thus will I thwart the process of the law,
For the blemish of so great a scandal sticks. 30

And, friend Maitreya, you must show your pride by not speaking too despondently.

*Maitreya.* How can a poor man help speaking despondently?

*Chārudatta.* Poor I am not, my friend. For I have a wife

Whose love outlasts my wealthy day;
In thee a friend through good and ill;
And truth that naught could take away:
Ah, this the poor man lacketh still. (28)

Go then, and after performing rites of purification, I will offer my morning prayer. [*Exeunt omnes.*

# ACT THE FOURTH

## MADANIKA AND SHARVILAKA

[*Enter a maid.*]

*Maid.*

I AM entrusted with a message for my mistress by her mother. Here is my mistress. She is gazing at a picture and is talking with Madanikā. I will go to her. [*She walks about. Then enter Vasantasenā, as described, and Madanikā.*]

*Vasantasenā.* Madanikā girl, is this portrait really like Chārudatta?

*Madanikā.* Very like.

*Vasantasenā.* How do you know?

*Madanikā.* Because my mistress' eyes are fastened so lovingly upon it.

*Vasantasenā.* Madanikā girl, do you say this because courtezan courtesy demands it?

*Madanikā.* But mistress, is the courtesy of a girl who lives in a courtezan's house, necessarily false?

*Vasantasenā.* Girl, courtezans meet so many kinds of men that they do learn a false courtesy.

*Madanikā.* But when the eyes of my mistress find such delight in a thing, and her heart too, what need is there to ask the reason?

*Vasantasenā.* But I should not like to have my friends laugh at me.

*Madanikā.* You need not be afraid. Women understand women.

*Maid.* [*Approaching.*] Mistress, your mother sends word that a covered cart is waiting at the side-door, and that you are to take a drive.

*Vasantasenā.* Tell me, is it Chārudatta who invites me?

*Maid.* Mistress, the man who sent ornaments worth ten thousand gold-pieces with the cart—

*Vasantasenā.* Is who?

*Maid.* Is the king's brother-in-law, Sansthānaka.

*Vasantasenā.* [*Indignantly.*] Go! and never come again on such an errand.

*Maid.* Do not be angry, mistress. I was only sent with the message.

*Vasantasenā.* But it is the message which makes me angry.

*Maid.* But what shall I tell your mother?

*Vasantasenā.* Tell my mother never to send me another such message, unless she wishes to kill me.

*Maid.* As you will. [*Exit.*] [*Enter Sharvilaka.*]

*Sharv.* Blame for my sin I laid upon the night;
I conquered sleep and watchmen of the king;
But darkness wanes, and in the sun's clear light
My light is like the moon's—a faded thing. 1

And again:

Whoever cast at me a passing look,
Or neared me, anxious, as they quickly ran,
All such my laden soul for foes mistook;
For sin it was wherein man's fear began. 2

Well, it was for Madanikā's sake that I did the deed of sin.

I paid no heed to any one who talked with serving-men;
The houses ruled by women-folk—these I avoided most;
And when policemen seemed to have me almost in their ken,
I stood stock-still and acted just exactly like a post.
A hundred such manœuvres did I constantly essay,
And by such means succeeded in turning night to day. 3

[*He walks about.*]

*Vasantasenā.* Girl, lay this picture on my sofa and come back at once with a fan.

*Madanikā.* Yes, mistress. [*Exit with the picture.*

*Sharvilaka.* This is Vasantasenā's house. I will enter. [*He does so.*]

I wonder where I can find Madanikā. [*Enter Madanikā with the fan. Sharvilaka discovers her.*] Ah, it is Madanikā.

Surpassing Madana[1] himself in charm,
She seems the bride of Love, in human guise;
Even while my heart the flames of passion harm,
She brings a sandal[2] coolness to my eyes. 4

Madanikā!

*Madanikā.* [*Discovers Sharvilaka.*] Oh, oh, oh, Sharvilaka! I am so glad, Sharvilaka. Where have you been?

*Sharvilaka.* I will tell you. [*They gaze at each other passionately.*]

*Vasantasenā.* How Madanikā lingers! I wonder where she is. [*She looks through a bull's-eye window.*] Why, there she stands, talking with a man. Her loving glance does not waver, and she gazes as if she would drink him in. I imagine he must be the man who wishes to make her free. Well, let her stay, let her stay. Never interrupt anybody's happiness. I will not call her.

*Madanikā.* Tell me, Sharvilaka. [*Sharvilaka looks about him uneasily.*] What is it, Sharvilaka? You seem uneasy.

*Sharvilaka.* I will tell you a secret. Are we alone?

*Madanikā.* Of course we are.

*Vasantasenā.* What! a deep secret? I will not listen.

*Sharvilaka.* Tell me, Madanikā. Will Vasantasenā take a price for your freedom?

*Vasantasenā.* The conversation has to do with me? Then I will hide behind this window and listen.

*Madanikā.* I asked my mistress about it, Sharvilaka, and she said that if she could have *her* way, she would free all her servants for nothing. But Sharvilaka, where did you find such a fortune that you can think of buying my freedom from my mistress?

*Sharvilaka.* A victim to my pauper plight,
And your sweet love to win,

[1] A name of Kāma, the god of love.

[2] Used as a refrigerant.

For you, my timid maid, last night
I did the deed of sin. 5

*Vasantasenā.* His face is tranquil. It would be troubled, if he had sinned.

*Madanikā.* Oh, Sharvilaka! For a mere nothing—for a woman—you have risked both things!

*Sharvilaka.* What things?

*Madanikā.* Your life and your character.

*Sharvilaka.* My foolish girl, fortune favors the brave.

*Madanikā.* Oh, Sharvilaka! Your character was without a stain. You did n't do anything *very* bad, did you, when for my sake you did the deed of sin?

*Sharv.* The gems that magnify a woman's charm,
As flowers the creeping plant, I do not harm.
I do not rob the Brahman of his pelf,
Nor seize the sacrificial gold myself.
I do not steal the baby from the nurse,
Simply because I need to fill my purse.
Even as a thief, I strive with main and might
For just distinction 'twixt the wrong and right. 6

And so you may tell Vasantasenā this:

These ornaments were made for you to don,
Or so it seems to me;
But as you love me, never put them on
Where other folks may see. 7

*Madanikā.* But Sharvilaka, ornaments that nobody may see, and a courtezan—the two things do not hang together. Give me the jewels. I want to see them.

*Sharvilaka.* Here they are. [*He gives them to her with some uneasiness.*]

*Madanikā.* [*Examining the jewels.*] It seems to me I have seen these before. Tell me. Where did you get them?

*Sharvilaka.* What does that matter to you, Madanikā? Take them.

*Madanikā.* [*Angrily.*] If you can't trust me, why do you wish to buy my freedom?

*Sharvilaka.* Well, this morning I heard in the merchants' quarter that the merchant Chārudatta—

[*Vasantasenā and Madanikā swoon.*]

*Sharvilaka.* Madanikā! Come to yourself! Why is it that now

Your figure seems to melt in limp despair,
Your eyes are wildly rolling here and there?
That when I come, sweet girl, to make you free,
You fall to trembling, not to pitying me? 8

*Madanikā.* [*Coming to herself.*] O you reckless man! When you did what you ought not to have done for my sake, you did n't kill anybody or hurt anybody in that house?

*Sharvilaka.* Madanikā, Sharvilaka does not strike a terrified man or a man asleep. I did not kill anybody nor hurt anybody.

*Madanikā.* Really?

*Sharvilaka.* Really.

*Vasantasenā.* [*Recovering consciousness.*] Ah, I breathe again.

*Madanikā.* Thank heaven!

*Sharvilaka.* [*Jealously.*] What does this "Thank heaven" mean, Madanikā?

I sinned for you, when love had made me pine,
Although my house was good since time began;
Love took my virtue, but my pride is mine.
*You* call me friend and love another man? 9

[*Meaningly.*] A noble youth is like a goodly tree;
His wealth, the fruit so fair;
The courtezan is like a bird; for she
Pecks him and leaves him bare. 10

Love is a fire, whose flame is lust,
Whose fuel is gallantry,

Wherein our youth and riches must
Thus sacrificèd be. 11

*Vasantasenā.* [*With a smile.*] His excitement is a little out of place.

*Sharvilaka.* Yes!

Those men are fools, it seems to me,
Who trust to women or to gold;
For gold and girls, 't is plain to see,
Are false as virgin snakes and cold. 12

Love not a woman; if you ever do,
She mocks at you, and plays the gay deceiver:
Yet if she loves you, you may love her too;
But if she does n't, leave her. 13

Too true it is that

A courtezan will laugh and cry for gold;
She trusts you not, but waits your trustful hour.
If virtue and a name are yours, then hold!
Avoid her as you would a graveyard flower. 14

And again:

As fickle as the billows of the sea,
Glowing no longer than the evening sky,
A woman takes your gold, then leaves you free;
You 're worthless, like cosmetics, when you 're dry. 15

Yes, women are indeed fickle.

One man perhaps may hold her heart in trust,
She lures another with coquettish eyes,
Sports with another in unseemly lust,
Another yet her body satisfies. 16

As some one has well said:

On mountain-tops no lotuses are grown;
The horse's yoke no ass will ever bear;
Rice never springs from seeds of barley sown;
A courtezan is not an honest fair. 17

Accursèd Chārudatta, you shall not live! [*He takes a few steps.*]

*Madanikā.* [*Seizing the hem of his garment.*] O you foolish man! Your anger is so ridiculous.

*Sharvilaka.* Ridiculous? how so?

*Madanikā.* Because these jewels belong to my mistress.

*Sharvilaka.* And what then?

*Madanikā.* And she left them with that gentleman.

*Sharvilaka.* What for?

*Madanikā.* [*Whispers.*] That 's why.

*Sharvilaka.* [*Sheepishly.*] Confound it!

The sun was hot one summer day;
I sought the shadow, there to stay:
Poor fool! the kindly branch to pay,
I stole its sheltering leaves away. 18

*Vasantasenā.* How sorry he seems. Surely, he did this thing in ignorance.

*Sharvilaka.* What is to be done now, Madanikā?

*Madanikā.* Your own wit should tell you that.

*Sharvilaka.* No. For you must remember,

Nature herself gives women wit;
Men learn from books a little bit. 19

*Madanikā.* Sharvilaka, if you will take my advice, restore the jewels to that righteous man.

*Sharvilaka.* But Madanikā, what if he should prosecute me?

*Madanikā.* No cruel heat comes from the moon.

*Vasantasenā.* Good, Madanikā, good!

*Sharvilaka.* Madanikā,

For what I did, I feel no grief nor fear;
Why tell me of this good man's virtues high?
Shame for my baseness touches me more near;
What can this king do to such rogues as I? 20

Nevertheless, your suggestion is inconsistent with prudence. You must discover some other plan.

*Madanikā.* Yes, there is another plan.

*Vasantasenā.* I wonder what it will be.

*Madanikā.* Pretend to be a servant of that gentleman, and give the jewels to my mistress.

*Sharvilaka.* And what then?

*Madanikā.* Then you are no thief, Chārudatta has discharged his obligation, and my mistress has her jewels.

*Sharvilaka.* But is n't this course too reckless?

*Madanikā.* I tell you, give them to her. Any other course is too reckless.

*Vasantasenā.* Good, Madanikā, good! Spoken like a free woman.

*Sharvilaka.* Risen at last is wisdom's light,
Because I followed after you;
When clouds obscure the moon by night,
'T is hard to find a guide so true. 21

*Madanikā.* Then you must wait here a moment in Kāma's shrine, while I tell my mistress that you have come.

*Sharvilaka.* I will.

*Madanikā.* [*Approaches Vasantasenā.*] Mistress, a Brahman has come from Chārudatta to see you.

*Vasantasenā.* But girl, how do you know that he comes from Chārudatta?

*Madanikā.* Should I not know my own, mistress?

*Vasantasenā.* [*Shaking her head and smiling. Aside.*] Splendid! [*Aloud.*] Bid him enter.

*Madanikā.* Yes, mistress. [*Approaching Sharvilaka.*] Enter, Sharvilaka.

*Sharvilaka.* [*Approaches. With some embarrassment.*] My greetings to you.

*Vasantasenā.* I salute you, sir. Pray be seated.

*Sharvilaka.* The merchant sends this message: "My house is so old that it is hard to keep this casket safe. Pray take it back." [*He gives it to Madanikā, and starts to leave.*]

*Vasantasenā.* Sir, will you undertake a return commission of mine?

*Sharvilaka.* [*Aside.*] Who will carry it? [*Aloud.*] And this commission is—

*Vasantasenā.* You will be good enough to accept Madanikā.

*Sharvilaka.* Madam, I do not quite understand.

*Vasantasenā.* But I do.

*Sharvilaka.* How so?

*Vasantasenā.* Chārudatta told me that I was to give Madanikā to the man who should return these jewels. You are therefore to understand that he makes you a present of her.

*Sharvilaka.* [*Aside.*] Ah, she sees through me. [*Aloud.*] Good, Chārudatta, good!

> On virtue only set your heart's desire;
> The righteous poor attain to heights whereto
> The wicked wealthy never may aspire. 22

And again:

> On virtue let the human heart be set;
> To virtue nothing serves as check or let.
> The moon, attaining unattainable, is led
> By virtue to her seat on Shiva's head. 23

*Vasantasenā.* Is my driver there? [*Enter a servant with a bullock-cart.*]

*Servant.* Mistress, the cart is ready.

*Vasantasenā.* Madanikā girl, you must show me a happy face. You are free. Enter the bullock-cart. But do not forget me.

*Madanikā.* [*Weeping.*] My mistress drives me away. [*She falls at her feet.*]

*Vasantasenā.* You are now the one to whom honor should be

paid.[1] Go then, enter the cart. But do not forget me.

*Sharvilaka.* Heaven bless you! and you, Madanikā,

Turn upon her a happy face,
And hail with bended head the grace
That gives you now the name of wife,
As a veil to keep you safe through life. 24

[*He enters the bullock-cart with Madanikā, and starts away.*]

*A voice behind the scenes.* Men! Men! We have the following orders from the chief of police: "A soothsayer has declared that a young herdsman named Aryaka is to become king. Trusting to this prophecy, and alarmed thereat, King Pālaka has taken him from his hamlet, and thrown him into strict confinement. Therefore be watchful, and every man at his post."

*Sharvilaka.* [*Listening.*] What! King Pālaka has imprisoned my good friend Aryaka? And here I am, a married man. Confound it! But no,

Two things alone—his friend, his wife—
Deserve man's love below;
A hundred brides may forfeit life
Ere he should suffer so. 25

Good! I will get out. [*He does so.*]

*Madanikā.* [*Folding her hands. Tearfully.*] My lord, if you must, at least bring me first to your parents.

*Sharvilaka.* Yes, my love, I will. I had the same thought in mind. [*To the servant.*] My good fellow, do you know the house of the merchant Rebhila?

*Servant.* Certainly.

*Sharvilaka.* Bring my wife thither.

*Servant.* Yes, sir.

*Madanikā.* If you desire it, dear. But dear, you must be very careful. [*Exit.*

[1] That is to say, You are now a legal wife, while I am still a courtezan.

*Sharvilaka.* Now as for me,

I'll rouse my kin, the kitchen cabinet,
Those high in fame by strength of good right arm,
And those who with the king's contempt have met,
And royal slaves, to save my friend from harm:
Like old Yaugandharāyana
For the good king Udayana. 26

And again:

My friend has causeless been confined
By wicked foes of timid kind;
I fly, I fly to free him soon,
Like the eclipse-oppressèd moon. [*Exit.*] 27

*Maid.* [*Entering.*] Mistress, I congratulate you. A Brahman has come with a message from Chārudatta.

*Vasantasenā.* Ah, this is a joyful day. Show him every mark of respect, girl, and have him conducted hither by one of the pages.

*Maid.* Yes, mistress. [*Exit.*

[*Enter Maitreya with a page.*]

*Maitreya.* Well! Rāvana, the king of the demons, travels with his chariot that they call the "Blossom." He earned it by his penances. Now I am a Brahman, and though I never performed any penances, I travel with another sort of a blossom—a woman of the town.

*Maid.* Sir, will you inspect our gateway.

*Maitreya.* [*Gazes admiringly.*] It has just been sprinkled and cleaned and received a coat of green. The threshold of it is pretty as a picture with the offerings of all sorts of fragrant flowers. It stretches up its head as if it wanted to peep into the sky. It is adorned with strings of jasmine garlands that hang down and toss about like the trunk of the heavenly elephant. It shines with its high ivory portal. It is lovely with any number of holiday banners that gleam red as great rubies and wave their coquettish fingers as they flutter in the breeze and seem to invite me to enter. Both sides are decorated with holiday water-jars of crystal, which are charming with their bright-green mango twigs, and are set at the foot of the pillars that sustain the portal. The doors are of gold, thickly set with diamonds as hard to pierce as a giant's breast. It actually wearies a poor devil's envy. Yes, Vasantasenā's house-door is a beautiful thing. Really, it forcibly challenges the attention of a man who does n't care about such things.

*Maid.* Come, sir, and enter the first court.

*Maitreya.* [*Enters and looks about.*] Well! Here in the first court are rows of balconies brilliant as the moon, or as sea-shells, or as lotus-stalks; whitened by handfuls of powder strewn over them; gleaming with golden stairways inlaid with all sorts of gems: they seem to gaze down on Ujjayinī with their round faces, the crystal windows, from which strings of pearls are dangling. The porter sits there and snoozes as comfortably as a professor. The crows which they tempt with rice-gruel and curdled milk will not eat the offering, because they can't distinguish it from the mortar. Show me the way, madam.

*Maid.* Come, sir, and enter the second court.

*Maitreya.* [*Enters and looks about.*] Well! Here in the second court the cart-bullocks are tied. They grow fat on mouthfuls of grass and pulse-stalks which are brought them, right and left, by everybody. Their horns are smeared with oil. And here is another, a buffalo, snorting like a gentleman insulted. And here is a ram[1] having his neck rubbed, like a prize-fighter after the fight. And here are others, horses having their manes put in shape. And here in a stall is another, a monkey, tied fast like a thief. [*He looks in another direction.*] And here is an elephant, taking from his drivers a cake of rice and drippings and oil. Show me the way, madam.

*Maid.* Come, sir, and enter the third court.

*Maitreya.* [*Enters and looks about.*] Well! Here in the third court

[1] "Rams in India are commonly trained to fight." WILSON.

are these seats, prepared for young gentlemen to sit on. A half-read book is lying on the gaming-table. And the table itself has its own dice, made out of gems. And here, again, are courtezans and old hangers-on at court, past masters in the war and peace of love, wandering about and holding in their fingers pictures painted in many colors. Show me the way, madam.

*Maid.* Come, sir, and enter the fourth court.

*Maitreya.* [*Enters and looks about.*] Well! Here in the fourth court the drums that maiden fingers beat are booming like the thunder; the cymbals are falling, as the stars fall from heaven when their merit is exhausted;[1] the pipe is discoursing music as sweet as the humming of bees. And here, again, is a lute that somebody is holding on his lap like a girl who is excited by jealousy and love, and he is stroking it with his fingers. And here, again, are courtezan girls that sing as charmingly as honey-drunken bees, and they are made to dance and recite a drama with love in it. And water-coolers are hanging in the windows so as to catch the breeze. Show me the way, madam.

*Maid.* Come, sir, and enter the fifth court.

*Maitreya.* [*Enters and looks about.*] Well! Here in the fifth court the overpowering smell of asafetida and oil is attractive enough to make a poor devil's mouth water. The kitchen is kept hot all the time, and the gusts of steam, laden with all sorts of good smells, seem like sighs issuing from its mouth-like doors. The smell of the preparation of all kinds of foods and sauces makes me smack my lips. And here, again, is a butcher's boy washing a mess of chitterlings as if it were an old loin-cloth. The cook is preparing every kind of food. Sweetmeats are being constructed, cakes are being baked. [*To himself.*] I wonder if I am to get a chance to wash my feet and an invitation to eat what I can hold. [*He looks in another direction.*] There are courtezans and bastard pages,

[1] Virtuous souls after death may become stars; but when their stellar happiness equals the sum of their acquired merit, they fall to earth again.

adorned with any number of jewels, just like Gandharvas[1] and Apsarases.[2] Really, this house is heaven. Tell me, who are you bastards anyway?

*Pages.* Why, we are bastard pages—

Petted in a stranger's court,
  Fed on stranger's food,
Stranger's money makes us sport—
  Not so very good.
Stranger women gave us birth,
  Stranger men begot;
Baby elephants in mirth,
  We 're a bastard lot. 28

*Maitreya.* Show me the way, madam.

*Maid.* Come, sir, and enter the sixth court.

*Maitreya.* [*Enters and looks about.*] Well! Here in the sixth court they are working in gold and jewels. The arches set with sapphires look as if they were the home of the rainbow. The jewelers are testing the lapis lazuli, the pearls, the corals, the topazes, the sapphires, the cat's-eyes, the rubies, the emeralds, and all the other kinds of gems. Rubies are being set in gold. Golden ornaments are being fashioned. Pearls are being strung on a red cord. Pieces of lapis lazuli are being cleverly polished. Shells are being pierced. Corals are being ground. Wet bundles of saffron are being dried. Musk is being moistened. Sandalwood is being ground to make sandal-water. Perfumes are being compounded. Betel-leaves and camphor are being given to courtezans and their lovers. Coquettish glances are being exchanged. Laughter is going on. Wine is being drunk incessantly with sounds of glee. Here are men-servants, here are maid-servants, and here are men who forget child and wife and money. When the courtezans, who have drunk the wine from the liquor-jars, give them the mitten, they—drink. Show me the way, madam.

[1] The choristers of heaven. [2] The nymphs of heaven.

*Maid.* Come, sir, and enter the seventh court.

*Maitreya.* [*Enters and looks about.*] Well! Here in the seventh court the mated doves are sitting comfortably in their snug dovecotes, billing and cooing and nothing else, and perfectly happy. And there is a parrot in a cage, chanting like a Brahman with a bellyful of curdled milk and rice. And here, again, is a talking thrush, chattering like a housemaid who spreads herself because somebody noticed her. A cuckoo, her throat still happy from tasting all sorts of fruit-syrups, is cooing like a procuress. Rows of cages are hanging from pegs. Quails are being egged on to fight. Partridges are being made to talk. Caged pigeons are being provoked. A tame peacock that looks as if he was adorned with all sorts of gems is dancing happily about, and as he flaps his wings, he seems to be fanning the roof which is distressed by the rays of the sun. [*He looks in another direction.*] Here are pairs of flamingos like moonbeams rolled into a ball, that wander about after pretty girls, as if they wanted to learn how to walk gracefully. And here, again, are tame cranes, walking around like ancient eunuchs. Well, well! This courtezan keeps a regular menagerie of birds. Really, the courtezan's house seems to me like Indra's heaven. Show me the way, madam.

*Maid.* Come, sir, and enter the eighth court.

*Maitreya.* [*Enters and looks about.*] Madam, who is this in the silk cloak, adorned with such astonishingly tautologous ornaments, who wanders about, stumbling and stretching his limbs?

*Maid.* Sir, this is my mistress' brother.

*Maitreya.* What sort of ascetic exercises does a man have to perform, in order to be born as Vasantasenā's brother? But no,

> He may be shiny, may be greasy,
> And perfumed may he be.
> And yet I warn you to go easy;
> He 's a graveyard champak-tree. 29

[*He looks in another direction.*] But madam, who is that in the expansive garment, sitting on the throne? She has shoes on her greasy feet.

*Maid.* Sir, that is my mistress' mother.

*Maitreya.* Lord! What an extensive belly the dirty old witch has got! I suppose they could n't put that superb portal on the house till after they had brought the idol in?

*Maid.* Rascal! You must not make fun of our mother so. She is pining away under a quartan ague.

*Maitreya.* [*Bursts out laughing.*] O thou blessèd quartan ague! Look thou upon a Brahman, even upon me, with this thy favor!

*Maid.* Rascal! May death strike you.

*Maitreya.* [*Bursts out laughing.*] Why, wench, a pot-belly like that is better dead.

> Drinking brandy, rum, and wine,
>   Mother fell extremely ill.
> If mother now should peak and pine,
>   A jackal-pack would have its fill. 30

Well, I have seen Vasantasenā's palace with its many incidents and its eight courts, and really, it seems as if I had seen the triple heaven in a nut-shell. I have n't the eloquence to praise it. Is this the house of a courtezan, or a piece of Kubera's [1] palace? Where 's your mistress?

*Maid.* She is here in the orchard. Enter, sir.

*Maitreya.* [*Enters and looks about.*] Well! What a beautiful orchard! There are any number of trees planted here, and they are covered with the most wonderful flowers. Silken swings are hung under the thick-set trees, just big enough for a girl to sit in. The golden jasmine, the shephālikā, the white jasmine, the jessamine, the navamallikā, the amaranth, the spring creeper, and all the other flowers have fallen of themselves, and really, it makes Indra's hea-

[1] The god of wealth.

ven look dingy. [*He looks in another direction.*] And the pond here looks like the morning twilight, for the lilies and red lotuses are as splendid as the rising sun. And again:

The ashoka-tree, whose twigs so merry
 And crimson flowers have just appeared,
Seems like a battling mercenary,
 With clotting crimson gore besmeared. 31

Good! Now where's your mistress?

*Maid.* If you would stop star-gazing, sir, you would see her.

*Maitreya.* [*Perceives Vasantasenā and approaches.*] Heaven bless you!

*Vasantasenā.* [*Speaking in Sanskrit.*[1]] Ah, Maitreya! [*Rising.*] You are very welcome. Here is a seat. Pray be seated.

*Maitreya.* When you are seated, madam. [*They both seat themselves.*]

*Vasantasenā.* Is the merchant's son well?

*Maitreya.* Well, madam.

*Vasantasenā.* Tell me, good Maitreya,

Do friends, like birds, yet seek a shelter free
Beneath the modest boughs of this fair tree,
Whose leaves are virtues, confidence its root,
Its blossoms honor, good its precious fruit? 32

*Maitreya.* [*Aside.*] A good description by a naughty woman. [*Aloud.*] They do, indeed.

*Vasantasenā.* Tell me, what is the purpose of your coming?

*Maitreya.* Listen, madam. The excellent Chārudatta folds his hands[2] and requests—

*Vasantasenā.* [*Folding her hands.*] And commands—

*Maitreya.* He says he imagined that that golden casket was his own and gambled it away. And nobody knows where the gambling-

[1] This shows the excellence of Vasantasenā's education. Women, as an almost invariable rule, speak Prākrit.

[2] A gesture of respectful entreaty.

master has gone, for he is employed in the king's business.

*Maid.* Mistress, I congratulate you. The gentleman has turned gambler.

*Vasantasenā.* [*Aside.*] It was stolen by a thief, and he is so proud that he says he gambled it away. I love him for that.

*Maitreya.* He requests that you will therefore be good enough to accept in its place this necklace of pearls.

*Vasantasenā.* [*Aside.*] Shall I show him the jewels? [*Reflecting.*] No, not yet.

*Maitreya.* Why don't you take this necklace?

*Vasantasenā.* [*Laughs and looks at her friend.*] Why should I not take the necklace, Maitreya? [*She takes it and lays it away. Aside.*] How is it possible that drops of honey fall from the mango-tree, even after its blossoms are gone? [*Aloud.*] Sir, pray tell the worthy gambler Chārudatta in my name that I shall pay him a visit this evening.

*Maitreya.* [*Aside.*] What else does she expect to get out of a visit to our house? [*Aloud.*] Madam, I will tell him—[*aside*] to have nothing more to do with this courtezan. [*Exit.*

*Vasantasenā.* Take these jewels, girl. Let us go and bring cheer to Chārudatta.

*Maid.* But mistress, see! An untimely storm is gathering.

*Vasant.* The clouds may come, the rain may fall forever,
The night may blacken in the sky above;
For this I care not, nor I will not waver;
My heart is journeying to him I love. 33

Take the necklace, girl, and come quickly. [*Exeunt omnes.*

## ACT THE FIFTH

### THE STORM

[*The love-lorn Chārudatta appears, seated.*]

*Chārudatta.* [*Looks up.*]

AN untimely storm[1] is gathering. For see!

The peacocks gaze and lift their fans on high;
The swans forget their purpose to depart;
The untimely storm afflicts the blackened sky,
And the wistful lover's heart. 1

And again:

The wet bull's belly wears no deeper dye;
In flashing lightning's golden mantle clad,
While cranes, his buglers, make the heaven glad,
The cloud, a second Vishnu,[2] mounts the sky. 2

And yet again:

As dark as Vishnu's form, with circling cranes
To trumpet him, instead of bugle strains,
And garmented in lightning's silken robe,
Approaches now the harbinger of rains. 3

When lightning's lamp is lit, the silver river
Impetuous falls from out the cloudy womb;
Like severed lace from heaven-cloaking gloom,
It gleams an instant, then is gone forever. 4

Like shoaling fishes, or like dolphins shy,
Or like to swans, toward heaven's vault that fly,
Like paired flamingos, male and mate together,
Like mighty pinnacles that tower on high,

[1] In Indian love-poetry, the rainy season is the time when lovers most ardently long to be united.

[2] In allusion to Vishnu's name, Krishna, "black."

In thousand forms the tumbling clouds embrace,
Though torn by winds, they gather, interlace,
And paint the ample canvas of the sky. 5

The sky is black as Dhritarāshtra's face;
Proud as the champion of Kuru's race,
The haughty peacock shrills his joy abroad;
The cuckoo, in Yudhishthira's sad case,
Is forced to wander if he would not die;
The swans must leave their forest-homes and fly,
Like Pāndu's sons, to seek an unknown place. 6

[*Reflecting.*] It is long since Maitreya went to visit Vasantasenā. And even yet he does not come. [*Enter Maitreya.*]

*Maitreya.* Confound the courtezan's avarice and her incivility! To think of her making so short a story of it! Over and over she repeats something about the affection she feels, and then without more ado she pockets the necklace. She is rich enough so that she might at least have said: "Good Maitreya, rest a little. You must not go until you have had a cup to drink." Confound the courtezan! I hope I 'll never set eyes on her again. [*Wearily.*] The proverb is right. "It is hard to find a lotus-plant without a root, a merchant who never cheats, a goldsmith who never steals, a village-gathering without a fight, and a courtezan without avarice." Well, I 'll find my friend and persuade him to have nothing more to do with this courtezan. [*He walks about until he discovers Chārudatta.*] Ah, my good friend is sitting in the orchard. I 'll go to him. [*Approaching.*] Heaven bless you! May happiness be yours.

*Chārudatta.* [*Looking up.*] Ah, my friend Maitreya has returned. You are very welcome, my friend. Pray be seated.

*Maitreya.* Thank you.

*Chārudatta.* Tell me of your errand, my friend.

*Maitreya.* My errand went all wrong.

*Chārudatta.* What! did she not accept the necklace?

*Maitreya.* How could we expect such a piece of luck? She put her lotus-tender hands to her brow,[1] and took it.

*Chārudatta.* Then why do you say "went wrong"?

*Maitreya.* Why not, when we lost a necklace that was the pride of the four seas for a cheap golden casket, that was stolen before we had a bite or a drink out of it?

*Chārudatta.* Not so, my friend.

She showed her trust in leaving us her treasure;
The price of confidence has no less measure. 7

*Maitreya.* Now look here! I have a second grievance. She tipped her friend the wink, covered her face with the hem of her dress, and laughed at me. And so, Brahman though I am, I hereby fall on my face before you and beg you not to have anything more to do with this courtezan. That sort of society does any amount of damage. A courtezan is like a pebble in your shoe. It hurts before you get rid of it. And one thing more, my friend. A courtezan, an elephant, a scribe, a mendicant friar, a swindler, and an ass—where these dwell, not even rogues are born.

*Chārudatta.* Oh, my friend, a truce to all your detraction! My poverty of itself prevents me. For consider:

The horse would gladly hasten here and there,
  But his legs fail him, for his breath departs.
So men's vain wishes wander everywhere,
  Then, weary grown, return into their hearts. 8

Then too, my friend:

If wealth is thine, the maid is thine,
  For maids are won by gold;

[*Aside.* And not by virtue cold. *Aloud.*]

But wealth is now no longer mine,
  And her I may not hold. 9

[1] A gesture of respect.

*Maitreya.* [*Looks down. Aside.*] From the way he looks up and sighs, I conclude that my effort to distract him has simply increased his longing. The proverb is right. "You can't reason with a lover." [*Aloud.*] Well, she told me to tell you that she would have to come here this evening. I suppose she is n't satisfied with the necklace and is coming to look for something else.

*Chārudatta.* Let her come, my friend. She shall not depart unsatisfied. [*Enter Kumbhīlaka.*]

*Kumbhīlaka.* Listen, good people.

The more it rains in sheets,
The more my skin gets wet;
The more the cold wind beats,
The more I shake and fret. 10

[*He bursts out laughing.*]

I make the sweet flute speak from seven holes,
I make the loud lute speak on seven strings;
In singing, I essay the donkey's rôles:
No god can match my music when he sings. 11

My mistress Vasantasenā said to me "Kumbhīlaka, go and tell Chārudatta that I am coming." So here I am, on my way to Chārudatta's house. [*He walks about, and, as he enters, discovers Chārudatta.*] Here is Chārudatta in the orchard. And here is that wretched jackanapes, too. Well, I'll go up to them. What! the orchard-gate is shut? Good! I'll give this jackanapes a hint. [*He throws lumps of mud.*]

*Maitreya.* Well! Who is this pelting me with mud, as if I were an apple-tree inside of a fence?

*Chārudatta.* Doubtless the pigeons that play on the roof of the garden-house.

*Maitreya.* Wait a minute, you confounded pigeon! With this stick I'll bring you down from the roof to the ground, like an over-ripe mango. [*He raises his stick and starts to run.*]

*Chārudatta.* [*Holding him back by the sacred cord.*] Sit down, my friend. What do you mean? Leave the poor pigeon alone with his mate.

*Kumbhīlaka.* What! he sees the pigeon and doesn't see me? Good! I'll hit him again with another lump of mud. [*He does so.*]

*Maitreya.* [*Looks about him.*] What! Kumbhīlaka? I'll be with you in a minute. [*He approaches and opens the gate.*] Well, Kumbhīlaka, come in. I'm glad to see you.

*Kumbhīlaka.* [*Enters.*] I salute you, sir.

*Maitreya.* Where do you come from, man, in this rain and darkness?

*Kumbhīlaka.* You see, she's here.

*Maitreya.* Who's she? Who's here?

*Kumbhīlaka.* She. See? She.

*Maitreya.* Look here, you son of a slave! What makes you sigh like a half-starved old beggar in a famine, with your "shesheshe"?

*Kumbhīlaka.* And what makes you hoot like an owl with your "whowhowho"?

*Maitreya.* All right. Tell me.

*Kumbhīlaka.* [*Aside.*] Suppose I say it this way. [*Aloud.*] I'll give you a riddle, man.

*Maitreya.* And I'll give you the answer with my foot on your bald spot.

*Kumbhīlaka.* Not till you've guessed it. In what season do the mango-trees blossom?

*Maitreya.* In summer, you jackass.

*Kumbhīlaka.* [*Laughing.*] Wrong!

*Maitreya.* [*Aside.*] What shall I say now? [*Reflecting.*] Good! I'll go and ask Chārudatta. [*Aloud.*] Just wait a moment. [*Approaching Chārudatta.*] My friend, I just wanted to ask you in what season the mango-trees blossom.

*Chārudatta.* You fool, in spring, in *vasanta.*

*Maitreya.* [*Returns to Kumbhīlaka.*] You fool, in spring, in *vasanta.*

*Kumbhīlaka.* Now I'll give you another. Who guards thriving villages?

*Maitreya.* Why, the guard.

*Kumbhīlaka.* [*Laughing.*] Wrong!

*Maitreya.* Well, I'm stuck. [*Reflecting.*] Good! I'll ask Chārudatta again. [*He returns and puts the question to Chārudatta.*]

*Chārudatta.* The army, my friend, the *senā.*

*Maitreya.* [*Comes back to Kumbhīlaka.*] The army, you jackass, the *senā.*

*Kumbhīlaka.* Now put the two together and say 'em fast.

*Maitreya.* Senā-vasanta.

*Kumbhīlaka.* Say it turned around.

*Maitreya.* [*Turns around.*] Senā-vasanta.

*Kumbhīlaka.* You fool! you jackanapes! Turn the parts of the thing around!

*Maitreya.* [*Turns his feet around.*] Senā-vasanta.

*Kumbhīlaka.* You fool! Turn the parts of the word around!

*Maitreya.* [*After reflection.*] Vasanta-senā.

*Kumbhīlaka.* She's here.

*Maitreya.* Then I must tell Chārudatta. [*Approaching.*] Well, Chārudatta, your creditor is here.

*Chārudatta.* How should a creditor come into my family?

*Maitreya.* Not in the family perhaps, but at the door. Vasantasenā is here.

*Chārudatta.* Why do you deceive me, my friend?

*Maitreya.* If you can't trust me, then ask Kumbhīlaka here. Kumbhīlaka, you jackass, come here.

*Kumbhīlaka.* [*Approaching.*] I salute you, sir.

*Chārudatta.* You are welcome, my good fellow. Tell me, is Vasantasenā really here?

*Kumbhīlaka.* Yes, she 's here. Vasantasenā is here.

*Chārudatta.* [*Joyfully.*] My good fellow, I have never let the bearer of welcome news go unrewarded. Take this as your recompense. [*He gives him his mantle.*]

*Kumbhīlaka.* [*Takes it and bows. Gleefully.*] I 'll tell my mistress. [*Exit.*

*Maitreya.* Do you see why she comes in a storm like this?

*Chārudatta.* I do not quite understand, my friend.

*Maitreya.* I know. She has an idea that the pearl necklace is cheap, and the golden casket expensive. She is n't satisfied, and she has come to look for something more.

*Chārudatta.* [*Aside.*] She shall not depart unsatisfied.

[*Then enter the love-lorn Vasantasenā, in a splendid garment, fit for a woman who goes to meet her lover, a maid with an umbrella, and the courtier.*]

*Courtier.* [*Referring to Vasantasenā.*]

Lakshmī[1] without the lotus-flower is she,
  Loveliest arrow of god Kāma's bow,[2]
The sweetest blossom on love's magic tree.
See how she moves, so gracefully and slow!
  In passion's hour she still loves modesty;
In her, good wives their dearest sorrow know.
When passion's drama shall enacted be,
  When on love's stage appears the passing show,
  A host of wanderers shall bend them low,
Glad to be slaves in such captivity. 12

[1] The goddess of wealth and beauty, usually represented with a lotus.

[2] Kāma's (Cupid's) arrows are flowers.

See, Vasantasenā, see!

The clouds hang drooping to the mountain peaks,
Like a maiden's heart, that distant lover seeks:
The peacocks startle, when the thunder booms,
And fan the heaven with all their jeweled plumes. 13

And again:

Mud-stained, and pelted by the streaming rain,
To drink the falling drops the frogs are fain;
Full-throated peacocks love's shrill passion show,
And nīpa flowers like brilliant candles glow;
Unfaithful clouds obscure the hostage moon,
Like knaves, unworthy of so dear a boon;
Like some poor maid of better breeding bare,
The impatient lightning rests not anywhere. 14

*Vasantasenā.*[1] Sir, what you say is most true. For

The night, an angry rival, bars my way;
Her thunders fain would check and hinder me:
"Fond fool! with him I love thou shalt not stay,
'T is I, 't is I, he loves," she seems to say,
"Nor from my swelling bosom shall he flee." 15

*Courtier.* Yes, yes. That is right. Scold the night.

*Vasantasenā.* And yet, sir, why scold one who is so ignorant of woman's nature? For you must remember:

The clouds may rain, may thunder ne'er so bold,
May flash the lightning from the sky above;
That woman little recks of heat or cold,
Who journeys to her love. 16

*Courtier.* But see, Vasantasenā! Another cloud,

Sped by the fickle fury of the air—
A flood of arrows in his rushing streams,
His drum, the roaring thunder's mighty blare,
His banner, living lightning's awful gleams—

[1] Throughout this scene, Vasantasenā's verses are in Sanskrit. Compare note 1 on page 73.

Rages within the sky, and shows him bold
'Mid beams that to the moon allegiance owe,
Like a hero-king within the hostile hold
Of his unwarlike foe. 17

*Vasantasenā.* True, true. And more than this:

As dark as elephants, these clouds alone
Fall like a cruel dart—
With streaks of lightning and with white birds strewn—
To wound my wretched heart.
But, oh, why should the heron, bird of doom,
With that perfidious sound[1]
Of "Rain! Rain! Rain!"—grim summons to the tomb
For her who spends her lonely hours in gloom—
Strew salt upon the wound? 18

*Courtier.* Very true, Vasantasenā. And yet again:

It seems as if the sky would take the guise
Of some fierce elephant to service bred;
The lightning like a waving streamer flies,
And white cranes serve to deck his mighty head. 19

*Vasantasenā.* But look, sir, look!

Clouds, black as wet tamāla-leaves, the ball
Of heaven hide from our sight;
Rain-smitten homes of ants decay and fall
Like beasts that arrows smite;
Like golden lamps within a lordly hall
Wander the lightnings bright;
As when men steal the wife of some base thrall,
Clouds rob the moon of light. 20

*Courtier.* See, Vasantasenā, see!

Clouds, harnessed in the lightning's gleams,
Like charging elephants dash by;

[1] The cry of the heron resembles the Sanskrit word for "rain." Indian love-poetry often paints the sorrow, even unto death, of her whose belovèd does not return before the rainy season.

At Indra's bidding, pour their streams,
Until with silver cords it seems
That earth is linked with sky. 21

And look yonder!

As herds of buffaloes the clouds are black;
The winds deny them ease;
They fly on lightning wings and little lack
Of seeming troubled seas.

Smitten with falling drops, the fragrant sod,
Upon whose bosom greenest grasses nod,
Seems pierced with pearls, each pearl an arrowy rod. 22

*Vasantasenā*. And here is yet another cloud.

The peacock's shrill-voiced cry
Implores it to draw nigh;
And ardent cranes on high
Embrace it lovingly.

The wistful swans espy
The lotus-sweeter sky;
The darkest colors lie
On heaven clingingly. 23

*Courtier*. True. For see!

A thousand lotuses that bloom by night,
A thousand blooming when the day is bright,
Nor close nor ope their eyes to heaven's sight;
There is no night nor day.

The face of heaven, thus shrouded in the night,
Is only for a single instant bright,
When momentary lightning gives us sight;
Else is it dark alway.

Now sleeps the world as still as in the night
Within the house of rain where naught is bright,

Where hosts of swollen clouds seem to our sight
  One covering veil of gray. 24

*Vasantasenā.* True. And see!

The stars are lost like mercies given
  To men of evil heart;
Like lonely-parted wives, the heaven
  Sees all her charms depart.
And, molten in the cruel heat
  Of Indra's bolt, it seems
As if the sky fell at our feet
  In liquid, flowing streams. 25

And yet again:

The clouds first darkly rise, then darkly fall,
Send forth their floods of rain, and thunder all;
Assuming postures strange and manifold,
Like men but newly blest with wealth untold. 26

*Courtier.* True.

The heaven is radiant with the lightning's glare;
  Its laughter is the cry of myriad cranes;
Its voice, the bolts that whistle through the air;
  Its dance, that bow whose arrows are the rains.
It staggers at the winds, and seems to smoke
With clouds, which form its black and snaky cloak. 27

*Vasantasenā.* O shameless, shameless sky!

To thunder thus, while I
To him I love draw nigh.
Why do thy thunders frighten me and pain?
Why am I seized upon by hands of rain? 28

O Indra, mighty Indra!

Did I then give thee of my love before,
That now thy clouds like mighty lions roar?
Ah no! Thou shouldst not send thy streaming rain,
To fill my journey to my love with pain. 29

Remember:

For Ahalyā's sweet sake thou once didst lie;
Thou knowest lover's pain.
As thou didst suffer then, now suffer I;
O cruel, cease thy rain. 30

And yet:

Thunder and rain and lighten hundredfold
Forth from thy sky above;
The woman canst thou not delay nor hold
Who journeys to her love. 31

Let thunders roar, for men were cruel ever;
But oh, thou maiden lightning! didst thou never
Know pains that maidens know? 32

*Courtier.* But mistress, do not scold the lightning. She is your friend,

This golden cord that trembles on the breast
Of great Airāvata;[1] upon the crest
Of rocky hills this banner all ablaze;
This lamp in Indra's palace; but most blest
As telling where your most belovèd stays. 33

*Vasantasenā.* And here, sir, is his house.

*Courtier.* You know all the arts, and need no instruction now. Yet love bids me prattle. When you enter here, you must not show yourself too angry.

Where anger is, there love is not;
Or no! except for anger hot,
There is no love.

Be angry! make him angry then!
Be kind! and make him kind again—
The man you love. 34

So much for that. Who is there? Let Chārudatta know, that

[1] The elephant of Indra. Indra is the god of the thunderstorm.

While clouds look beautiful, and in the hour
Fragrant with nīpa and kadamba flower,
She comes to see her lover, very wet,
With dripping locks, but pleased and loving yet.
Though lightning and though thunder terrifies,
She comes to see you; 't is for you she sighs.
The mud still soils the anklets on her feet,
But in a moment she will have them sweet. 35

*Chārudatta.* [*Listening.*] My friend, pray discover what this means.

*Maitreya.* Yes, sir. [*He approaches Vasantasenā. Respectfully.*] Heaven bless you!

*Vasantasenā.* I salute you, sir. I am very glad to see you. [*To the courtier.*] Sir, the maid with the umbrella is at your service.

*Courtier.* [*Aside.*] A very clever way to get rid of me. [*Aloud.*] Thank you. And mistress Vasantasenā,

Pride and tricks and lies and fraud
  Are in your face;
False playground of the lustful god,
  Such is your face;
The wench's stock in trade, in fine,
Epitome of joys divine,
  I mean, your face—
For sale! the price is courtesy.
I trust you 'll find a man to buy
  Your face. [*Exit.*] 36

*Vasantasenā.* Good Maitreya, where is your gambler?

*Maitreya.* [*Aside.*] "Gambler"? Ah, she 's paying a compliment to my friend. [*Aloud.*] Madam, here he is in the dry orchard.

*Vasantasenā.* But sir, what do you call a dry orchard?

*Maitreya.* Madam, it 's a place where there 's nothing to eat or drink. [*Vasantasenā smiles.*] Pray enter, madam.

*Vasantasenā.* [*Aside to her maid.*] What shall I say when I enter?

*Maid.* "Gambler, what luck this evening?"

*Vasantasenā.* Shall I dare to say it?

*Maid.* When the time comes, it will say itself.

*Maitreya.* Enter, madam.

*Vasantasenā.* [*Enters, approaches Chārudatta, and strikes him with the flowers which she holds.*] Well, gambler, what luck this evening?

*Chārudatta.* [*Discovers her.*] Ah, Vasantasenā is here. [*He rises joyfully.*] Oh, my belovèd,

My evenings pass in watching ever,
  My nights from sighs are never free;
This evening cannot else than sever—
  In bringing you—my grief and me. 37

You are very, very welcome. Here is a seat. Pray be seated.

*Maitreya.* Here is a seat. Be seated, madam. [*Vasantasenā sits, then the others.*]

*Chārudatta.* But see, my friend,

The dripping flower that decks her ear, droops down,
  And one sweet breast
Anointed is, like a prince who wears the crown,
  With ointment blest. 38

My friend, Vasantasenā's garments are wet. Let other, and most beautiful, garments be brought.

*Maitreya.* Yes, sir.

*Maid.* Good Maitreya, do you stay here. I will wait upon my mistress. [*She does so.*]

*Maitreya.* [*Aside to Chārudatta.*] My friend, I 'd just like to ask the lady a question.

*Chārudatta.* Then do so.

*Maitreya.* [*Aloud.*] Madam, what made you come here, when it is so stormy and dark that you can't see the moon?

*Maid.* Mistress, the Brahman is very plain-spoken.

*Vasantasenā.* You might better call him clever.

*Maid.* My mistress came to ask how much that pearl necklace is worth.

*Maitreya.* [*Aside to Chārudatta.*] There! I told you so. She thinks the pearl necklace is cheap, and the golden casket is expensive. She is n't satisfied. She has come to look for something more.

*Maid.* For my mistress imagined that it was her own, and gambled it away. And nobody knows where the gambling-master has gone, for he is employed in the king's business.

*Maitreya.* Madam, you are simply repeating what somebody said before.

*Maid.* While we are looking for him, pray take this golden casket. [*She displays the casket. Maitreya hesitates.*] Sir, you examine it very closely. Did you ever see it before?

*Maitreya.* No, madam, but the skilful workmanship captivates the eye.

*Maid.* Your eyes deceive you, sir. This *is* the golden casket.

*Maitreya.* [*Joyfully.*] Well, my friend, here is the golden casket, the very one that thieves stole from our house.

*Chārudatta.* My friend,

> The artifice we tried before,
> Her stolen treasure to restore,
> Is practised now on us. But no,
> I cannot think 't is really so. 39

*Maitreya.* But it is so. I swear it on my Brahmanhood.

*Chārudatta.* This is welcome news.

*Maitreya.* [*Aside to Chārudatta.*] I 'm going to ask where they found it.

*Chārudatta.* I see no harm in that.

*Maitreya.* [*Whispers in the maid's ear.*] There!

*Maid.* [*Whispers in Maitreya's ear.*] So there!

*Chārudatta.* What is it? and why are we left out?

*Maitreya.* [*Whispers in Chārudatta's ear.*] So there!

*Chārudatta.* My good girl, is this really the same golden casket?

*Maid.* Yes, sir, the very same.

*Chārudatta.* My good girl, I have never let the bearer of welcome news go unrewarded. Take this ring as your recompense. [*He looks at his finger, notices that the ring is gone, and betrays his embarrassment.*]

*Vasantasenā.* [*To herself.*] I love you for that.

*Chārudatta.* [*Aside to Maitreya.*] Alas,

When in this world a man has lost his all,
  Why should he set his heart on longer life?
His angers and his favors fruitless fall,
  His purposes and powers are all at strife. 40

Like wingless birds, dry pools, or withered trees,
Like fangless snakes—the poor are like to these. 41

Like man-deserted houses, blasted trees,
Like empty wells—the poor are like to these.
For them no pleasant hours serve happy ends;
They are forgotten of their sometime friends. 42

*Maitreya.* But you must not grieve thus beyond reason. [*He bursts out laughing. Aloud.*] Madam, please give me back my bath-clout.

*Vasantasenā.* Chārudatta, it was not right that you should show your distrust of me by sending me this pearl necklace.

*Chārudatta.* [*With an embarrassed smile.*] But remember, Vasantasenā,

Who will believe the truth?
  Suspicion now is sure.
This world will show no ruth
  To the inglorious poor. 43

*Maitreya.* Tell me, girl, are you going to sleep here to-night?.

*Maid.* [*Laughing.*] But good Maitreya, you show yourself most remarkably plain-spoken now.

*Maitreya.* See, my friend, the rain enters again in great streams, as if it wanted to drive people away when they are sitting comfortably together.

*Chārudatta.* You are quite right.

The falling waters pierce the cloud,
As lotus-shoots the soil;
And tears the face of heaven shroud,
Who weeps the moon's vain toil. 44

And again:

In streams as pure as thoughts to good men given,
But merciless as darts that Arjun hurls,
And black as Baladeva's cloak, the heaven
Seems to pour out all Indra's hoarded pearls. 45

See, my belovèd, see!

The heaven is painted with the blackest dye,
And fanned by cool and fragrant evening airs;
Red lightning, glad in union, clasps the sky
With voluntary arms, and shows on high
The love that maiden heart to lover bears. 46

[*Vasantasenā betrays her passion, and throws her arms about Chārudatta. Chārudatta feels her touch, and embraces her.*]

*Chārudatta.* More grimly yet, O thunder, boom;
For by thy grace and power
My love-distracted limbs now bloom
Like the kadamba flower.
Her dear touch all my being thrills,
And love my inmost spirit fills. 47

*Maitreya.* Confound you, storm! You are no gentleman, to frighten the lady with the lightning.

*Chārudatta.* Do not rebuke the storm, my friend.

Let ceaseless rain a hundred years endure,
The lightning quiver, and the thunder peal;
For what I deemed impossible is sure:
Her dear-loved arms about my neck I feel. 48

And oh, my friend,

He only knows what riches are,
Whose love comes to him from afar,
Whose arms that dearest form enfold,
While yet with rain 't is wet and cold. 49

Vasantasenā, my belovèd,

The masonry is shaken; and so old
The awning, that 't will not much longer hold.
Heavy with water is the painted wall,
From which dissolving bits of mortar fall. 50

[*He looks up.*] The rainbow! See, my belovèd, see!

See how they yawn, the cloudy jaws of heaven,
As by a tongue, by forkèd lightning riven;
And to the sky great Indra's fiery bow
In lieu of high-uplifted arms is given. 51

Come, let us seek a shelter. [*He rises and walks about.*]

On palm-trees shrill,
On thickets still,
On boulders dashing,
On waters splashing,
Like a lute that, smitten, sings,
The rainy music rings. 52

[*Exeunt omnes.*

# ACT THE SIXTH

## THE SWAPPING OF THE BULLOCK-CARTS

[*Enter a maid.*]

*Maid.*

ISN'T my mistress awake yet? Well, I must go in and wake her. [*She walks about. Vasantasenā appears, dressed, but still asleep. The maid discovers her.*] It is time to get up, mistress. The morning is here.

*Vasantasenā.* [*Awakening.*] What! is the night over? is it morning?

*Maid.* For us it is morning. But for my mistress it appears to be night still.

*Vasantasenā.* But girl, where is your gambler?

*Maid.* Mistress, after giving Vardhamānaka his orders, Chārudatta went to the old garden Pushpakaranda.

*Vasantasenā.* What orders?

*Maid.* To have the bullock-cart ready before daylight; for, he said, Vasantasenā was to come—

*Vasantasenā.* Where, girl?

*Maid.* Where Chārudatta is.

*Vasantasenā.* [*Embraces the maid.*] I did not have a good look at him in the evening. But to-day I shall see him face to face. Tell me, girl. Have I found my way into the inner court?

*Maid.* You have found your way not only into the inner court, but into the heart of every one who lives here.

*Vasantasenā.* Tell me, are Chārudatta's servants vexed?

*Maid.* They will be.

*Vasantasenā.* When?

*Maid.* When my mistress goes away.

*Vasantasenā.* But not so much as I shall be. [*Persuasively.*] Here, girl, take this pearl necklace. You must go and give it to my lady sister, his good wife. And give her this message: "Worthy Chārudatta's virtues have won me, made me his slave, and therefore your slave also. And so I hope that these pearls may adorn your neck."

*Maid.* But mistress, Chārudatta will be angry with you.

*Vasantasenā.* Go. He will not be angry.

*Maid.* [*Takes the necklace.*] Yes, mistress. [*She goes out, then returns.*] Mistress, his lady wife says that her lord made you a present of it, and it would not be right for her to accept it. And further, that you are to know that her lord and husband is her most excellent adornment.

[*Enter Radanikā, with Chārudatta's little son.*]

*Radanikā.* Come, dear, let 's play with your little cart.

*Rohasena.* [*Peevishly.*] I don't like this little clay cart, Radanikā. Give me my gold cart.

*Radanikā.* [*Sighing wearily.*] How should we have anything to do with gold now, my child? When your papa is rich again, then you shall have a gold cart to play with. But I 'll amuse him by taking him to see Vasantasenā. [*She approaches Vasantasenā.*] Mistress, my service to you.

*Vasantasenā.* I am glad to see you, Radanikā. But whose little boy is this? He wears no ornaments, yet his dear little face makes my heart happy.

*Radanikā.* This is Chārudatta's son, Rohasena.

*Vasantasenā.* [*Stretches out her arms.*] Come, my boy, and put your little arms around me. [*She takes him on her lap.*] He looks just like his father.

*Radanikā.* More than looks like him, he *is* like him. At least I think so. His father is perfectly devoted to him.

*Vasantasenā.* But what is he crying about?

*Radanikā.* He used to play with a gold cart that belongs to the son of a neighbor. But that was taken away, and when he asked for it, I made him this little clay cart. But when I gave it to him, he said "I don't like this little clay cart, Radanikā. Give me my gold cart."

*Vasantasenā.* Oh, dear! To think that this little fellow has to suffer because others are wealthy. Ah, mighty Fate! the destinies of men, uncertain as the water-drops which fall upon a lotus-leaf, seem to thee but playthings! [*Tearfully.*] Don't cry, my child. You shall have a gold cart to play with.

*Rohasena.* Who is she, Radanikā?

*Vasantasenā.* A slave of your father's, won by his virtues.

*Radanikā.* My child, the lady is your mother.

*Rohasena.* That's a lie, Radanikā. If the lady is my mother, why does she wear those pretty ornaments?

*Vasantasenā.* My child, your innocent lips can say terrible things. [*She removes her ornaments. Weeping.*] Now I am your mother. You shall take these ornaments and have a gold cart made for you.

*Rohasena.* Go away! I won't take them. You're crying.

*Vasantasenā.* [*Wiping away her tears.*] I'll not cry, dear. There! go and play. [*She fills the clay cart with her jewels.*] There, dear, you must have a little gold cart made for you.

[*Exit Radanikā, with Rohasena.*

[*Enter Vardhamānaka, driving a bullock-cart.*]

*Vardhamānaka.* Radanikā, Radanikā! Tell mistress Vasantasenā that the covered cart is standing ready at the side-door.

*Radanikā.* [*Entering.*] Mistress, Vardhamānaka is here, and he says that the cart is waiting at the side-door.

*Vasantasenā.* He must wait a minute, girl, while I get ready.

*Rad.* Wait a minute, Vardhamānaka, while she gets ready. [*Exit.*

*Vardhamānaka.* Hello, I've forgotten the cushion. I must go and get it. But the nose-rope makes the bullocks skittish. I suppose I had better take the cart along with me. [*Exit.*

*Vasantasenā.* Bring me my things, girl. I must make myself ready. [*She does so.*]

[*Enter, driving a bullock-cart, Sthāvaraka, servant to Sansthānaka.*]

*Sthāvaraka.* Sansthānaka, the king's brother-in-law, said to me "Take a bullock-cart, Sthāvaraka, and come as quick as you can to the old garden Pushpakaranda." Well, I 'm on my way there. Get up, bullocks, get up! [*He drives about and looks around.*] Why, the road is blocked with villagers' carts. What am I to do now? [*Haughtily.*] Get out of my way, you! Get out of my way! [*He listens.*] What 's that? you want to know whose cart this is? This cart belongs to Sansthānaka, the king's brother-in-law. So get out of my way—and this minute, too! [*He looks about.*] Why, here 's a man going in the other direction as fast as he can. He is trying to hide like a runaway gambler, and he looks at me as if I were the gambling-master. I wonder who he is. But then, what business is it of mine? I must get there as soon as I can. Get out of my way, you villagers, get out of my way! What 's that? you want me to wait a minute and put a shoulder to your wheel? Confound you! A brave man like me, that serves Sansthānaka, the king's brother-in-law, put a shoulder to your wheel? After all, the poor fellow is quite alone. I 'll do it. I 'll stop my cart at the side-door to Chārudatta's orchard. [*He does so.*] I 'm coming! [*Exit.*

*Maid.* Mistress, I think I hear the sound of wheels. The cart must be here.

*Vasantasenā.* Come, girl. My heart grows impatient. Go with me to the side-door.

*Maid.* Follow me, mistress.

*Vasantasenā.* [*Walks about.*] You have earned a rest, girl.

*Maid.* Thank you, mistress. [*Exit.*

*Vasantasenā.* [*Feels her right eye twitch*[1] *as she enters the cart.*]

[1] A bad omen, in the case of a woman.

Why should my right eye twitch now? But the sight of Chārudatta will smooth away the bad omen. [*Enter Sthāvaraka.*]

*Sthāvaraka.* I've cleared the carts out of the way, and now I'll go ahead. [*He mounts and drives away. To himself.*] The cart has grown heavy. But I suppose it only seems so, because I got tired helping them with that wheel. Well, I'll go along. Get up, bullocks, get up!

*A voice behind the scenes.* Police! Police! Every man at his post! The young herdsman has just broken jail, killed the jailer, broken his fetters, escaped, and run away. Catch him! Catch him!

[*Enter, in excited haste, Aryaka, an iron chain on one foot. Covering his face, he walks about.*]

*Sthāvaraka.* [*To himself.*] There is great excitement in the city. I must get out of the way as fast as I possibly can. [*Exit.*

*Aryaka.* I leave behind me that accursèd sea
Of human woe and human misery,
The prison of the king.
Like elephants that break their chains and flee,
I drag a fettered foot most painfully
In flight and wandering. 1

King Pālaka was frightened by a prophecy, took me from the hamlet where I lived, fettered me, and thrust me into a solitary cell, there to await my death. But with the help of my good friend Sharvilaka I escaped. [*He sheds tears.*]

If such my fate, no sin is mine at least,
That he should cage me like a savage beast.
A man may fight with kings, though not with fate—
And yet, can helpless men contend with great? 2

Whither shall I go with my wretchedness? [*He looks about.*] Here is the house of some good man who has n't locked the side-door.

The house is old, the door without a lock,
The hinges all awry.

Some man, no doubt, who feels misfortune's shock
As cruelly as I. 3

I will enter here and wait.

*A voice behind the scenes.* Get up, bullocks, get up!

*Aryaka.* [*Listening.*] Ah, a bullock-cart is coming this way.

If this should prove to be a picnic rig,
Its occupants not peevishly inclined;
Some noble lady's waiting carriage trig;
Or rich man's coach, that leaves the town behind—
And if it empty be, fate proving kind,
'T would seem a godsend to my anxious mind. 4

[*Enter Vardhamānaka with the bullock-cart.*]

*Vardhamānaka.* There, I 've got the cushion. Radanikā, tell mistress Vasantasenā that the cart is ready and waiting for her to get in and drive to the old garden Pushpakaranda.

*Aryaka.* [*Listening.*] This is a courtezan's cart, going out of the city. Good, I 'll climb in. [*He approaches cautiously.*]

*Vardhamānaka.* [*Hears him coming.*] Ah, the tinkling of ankle-rings! The lady is here. Mistress, the nose-rope makes the bullocks skittish. You had better climb in behind. [*Aryaka does so.*] The ankle-rings tinkle only when the feet are moving, and the sound has ceased. Besides, the cart has grown heavy. I am sure the lady must have climbed in by this time. I 'll go ahead. Get up, bullocks, get up! [*He drives about. Enter Vīraka.*]

*Vīraka.* Come, come! Jaya, Jayamāna, Chandanaka, Mangala, Phullabhadra, and the rest of you!

So calm, when the herdsman, slipping his tether,
Breaks jail and the heart of the king together? 5

Here! You stand at the east gate of the main street, you at the west, you at the south, you at the north. I 'll climb up the broken wall here with Chandanaka and take a look. Come on, Chandanaka, come on! This way! [*Enter Chandanaka, in excitement.*]

*Chandanaka.* Come, come! Vīraka, Vishalya, Bhīmāngada, Dandakāla, Dandashūra, and the rest of you!

Come quick, my reliables! Work! Now begin!
Lest the old king go out, and a new king come in. 6
Search gardens, and dives, and the town, and the street,
The market, the hamlet, wherever you meet 7
With what looks suspicious. Now, Vīraka, say,
Who saved the young herdsman that just broke away? 8
Who was born when the sun in his eighth mansion stood,
Or the moon in her fourth, or when Jupiter could
Be seen in his sixth, or when Saturn was resting
In his ninth, in her sixth house when Venus was nesting,
Or Mars in his fifth?[1] Who will dare to be giving
The herdsman protection, while I am still living? 9, 10

*Vīraka.* Chandanaka, you mercenary!

I swear on your heart, he 's been long out of prison,
For the herdsman escaped ere the sun was half risen. 11

*Vardhamānaka.* Get up, bullocks, get up!

*Chandanaka.* [*Discovers him.*] Look, man, look!

A covered cart is moving in the middle of the road;
Investigate it, whose it is, and where it takes its load! 12

*Vīraka.* [*Discovers him.*] Here, driver, stop your cart! Whose cart is this? who is in it? where is it going?

*Vardhamānaka.* This is Chārudatta's cart. Mistress Vasantasenā is in it. I am taking her to the old garden Pushpakaranda to meet Chārudatta.

*Vīraka.* [*Approaches Chandanaka.*] The driver says it is Chārudatta's cart; that Vasantasenā is in it; that he is taking her to the old garden Pushpakaranda.

*Chandanaka.* Then let it pass.

*Vīraka.* Without inspection?

[1] Lallādīkshita says that these horoscopes indicate respectively distress, colic, stupidity, poverty, sorrow, destruction.

*Chandanaka.* Certainly.

*Vīraka.* On whose authority?

*Chandanaka.* On Chārudatta's.

*Vīraka.* Who is Chārudatta, or who is Vasantasenā, that the cart should pass without inspection?

*Chandanaka.* Don't you know Chārudatta, man? nor Vasantasenā? If you don't know Chārudatta, nor Vasantasenā, then you don't know the moon in heaven, nor the moonlight.

Who does n't know this moon of goodness, virtue's lotus-
  flower,
This gem of four broad seas, this savior in man's luckless
  hour? 13
These two are wholly worshipful, our city's ornaments,
Vasantasenā, Chārudatta, sea of excellence. 14

*Vīraka.* Well, well, Chandanaka! Chārudatta? Vasantasenā?
I know them perfectly, as well as I know anything;
But I do not know my father when I 'm serving of my king. 15

*Aryaka.* [*To himself.*] In a former existence the one must have been my enemy, the other my kinsman. For see!

Their business is the same; their ways
  Unlike, and their desire:
Like flames that gladden wedding days,
  And flames upon the pyre. 16

*Chandanaka.* You are a most careful captain whom the king trusts. I am holding the bullocks. Make your inspection.

*Vīraka.* You too are a corporal whom the king trusts. Make the inspection yourself.

*Chandanaka.* If I make the inspection, that 's just the same as if you had made it?

*Vīraka.* If you make the inspection, that 's just the same as if King Pālaka had made it.

*Chandanaka.* Lift the pole, man! [*Vardhamānaka does so.*]

*Aryaka.* [*To himself.*] Are the policemen about to inspect me? And I have no sword, worse luck! But at least,

Bold Bhīma's spirit I will show;
My arm shall be my sword.
Better a warrior's death than woe
That cells and chains afford. 17

But the time to use force has not yet come. [*Chandanaka enters the cart and looks about.*] I seek your protection.

*Chandanaka.* [*Speaking in Sanskrit.*] He who seeks protection shall be safe.

*Aryaka.* Whene'er he fight, that man will suffer hurts,
Will be abandoned of his friends and kin,
Becomes a mock forever, who deserts
One seeking aid; 't is an unpardoned sin. 18

*Chandanaka.* What! the herdsman Aryaka? Like a bird that flees from a hawk, he has fallen into the hand of the fowler. [*Reflecting.*] He is no sinner, this man who seeks my protection and sits in Chārudatta's cart. Besides, he is the friend of good Sharvilaka, who saved my life. On the other hand, there are the king's orders. What is a man to do in a case like this? Well, what must be, must be. I promised him my protection just now.

He who gives aid to frightened men,
And joys his neighbor's ills to cure,
If he must die, he dies; but then,
His reputation is secure. 19

[*He gets down uneasily.*] I saw the gentleman—[*correcting himself*] I mean, the lady Vasantasenā, and she says "Is it proper, is it gentlemanly, when I am going to visit Chārudatta, to insult me on the highway?"

*Vīraka.* Chandanaka, I have my suspicions.

*Chandanaka.* Suspicions? How so?

*Vīr.* You gurgled in your craven throat; it seems a trifle shady.
You said "I saw the gentleman," and then "I saw the lady."

That 's why I 'm not satisfied.

*Chandanaka.* What 's the matter with you, man? We southerners don't speak plain. We know a thousand dialects of the barbarians—the Khashas, the Khattis, the Kadas, the Kadatthobilas, the Karnātas, the Karnas, the Prāvaranas, the Drāvidas, the Cholas, the Chīnas, the Barbaras, the Kheras, the Khānas, the Mukhas, the Madhughātas, and all the rest of 'em, and it all depends on the way we feel whether we say "he" or "she," "gentleman" or "lady."

*Vīraka.* Can't I have a look, too? It 's the king's orders. And the king trusts me.

*Chandanaka.* I suppose the king does n't trust *me!*

*Vīraka.* Is n't it His Majesty's command?

*Chandanaka.* [*Aside.*] If people knew that the good herdsman escaped in Chārudatta's cart, then the king would make Chārudatta suffer for it. What 's to be done? [*Reflecting.*] I 'll stir up a quarrel the way they do down in the Carnatic. [*Aloud.*] Well, Vīraka, I made one inspection myself—my name is Chandanaka—and you want to do it over again. Who are you?

*Vīraka.* Confound it! Who are you, anyway?

*Chandanaka.* An honorable and highly respectable person, and you don't remember your own family.

*Vīraka.* [*Angrily.*] Confound you! What is my family?

*Chandanaka.* Who speaks of such things?

*Vīraka.* Speak!

*Chandanaka.* I think I 'd better not.

I know your family, but I won't say;
'T would not be modest, such things to betray;
What good 's a rotten apple anyway? 21

*Vīraka.* Speak, speak! [*Chandanaka makes a significant gesture.*] Confound you! What does that mean?

*Chand.* A broken whetstone in one hand—a thing
That looks like scissors in the other wing—
To trim the scrubby beards that curl and cling,
And you—why, you 're a captain of the king! 22

*Vīraka.* Well, Chandanaka, you highly respectable person, you don't remember your own family either.

*Chandanaka.* Tell me. What is the family I belong to, I, Chandanaka, pure as the moon?

*Vīraka.* Who speaks of such things?

*Chandanaka.* Speak, speak! [*Vīraka makes a significant gesture.*] Confound you! What does that mean?

*Vīraka.* Listen.

Your house is pure; your father is a drum,
Your mother is a kettledrum, you scum!
Your brother is a tambourine—tum, tum!
And you—why, you 're a captain of the king! 23

*Chandanaka.* [*Wrathfully.*] I, Chandanaka, a tanner! You can look at the cart.

*Vīraka.* You! driver! turn the cart around. I want to look in. [*Vardhamānaka does so. Vīraka starts to climb in. Chandanaka seizes him violently by the hair, throws him down, and kicks him.*]

*Vīraka.* [*Rising. Wrathfully.*] Confound you! I was peaceably going about the king's business, when you seized me violently by the hair and kicked me. So listen! If I don't have you drawn and quartered in the middle of the court-room, my name 's not Vīraka.

*Chandanaka.* All right. Go to court or to a hall of justice. What do I care for a puppy like you?

*Vīraka.* I will. [*Exit.*

*Chandanaka.* [*Looks about him.*] Go on, driver, go on! If anybody asks you, just say "The cart has been inspected by Chandanaka and Vīraka." Mistress Vasantasenā, let me give you a passport. [*He hands Aryaka a sword.*]

*Aryaka.* [*Takes it. Joyfully to himself.*]

A sword, a sword! My right eye twitches fast.[1]
Now all is well, and I am safe at last. 24

*Chandanaka.* Madam,

As I have given you a passage free,
So may I live within your memory.
To utter this, no selfish thoughts could move;
Ah no, I speak in plenitude of love. 25

*Aryaka.* Chandanaka is rich in virtues pure;
My friend is he—Fate willed it—true and tried.
I 'll not forget Chandanaka, be sure,
What time the oracle is justified. 26

*Chand.* May Shiva, Vishnu, Brahma, Three in One,
Protect thee, and the Moon, and blessèd Sun;
Slay all thy foes, as mighty Pārvatī
Slew Shumbha and Nishumbha—fearfully. 27

[*Exit Vardhamānaka, with the bullock-cart. Chandanaka looks toward the back of the stage.*] Aha! As he goes away, my good friend Sharvilaka is following him. Well, I 've made an enemy of Vīraka, the chief constable and the king's favorite; so I think I too had better be following him, with all my sons and brothers.

[*Exit.*

[1] A good omen, in the case of a man.

## ACT THE SEVENTH

### ARYAKA'S ESCAPE

[*Enter Chārudatta and Maitreya.*]

*Maitreya.*

HOW beautiful the old garden Pushpakaranda is.

*Chārudatta.* You are quite right, my friend. For see!

The trees, like merchants, show their wares;
Each several tree his blossoms bears,
While bees, like officers, are flitting,
To take from each what toll is fitting. 1

*Maitreya.* This simple stone is very attractive. Pray be seated.

*Chārudatta.* [*Seats himself.*] How Vardhamānaka lingers, my friend!

*Maitreya.* I told Vardhamānaka to bring Vasantasenā and come as quickly as he could.

*Chārudatta.* Why then does he linger?

Is he delayed by some slow-moving load?
  Has he returned with broken wheel or traces?
Obstructions bid him seek another road?
  His bullocks, or himself, choose these slow paces? 2

[*Enter Vardhamānaka with the bullock-cart, in which Aryaka lies hidden.*]

*Vardhamānaka.* Get up, bullocks, get up!

*Aryaka.* [*Aside.*]

And still I fear the spies that serve the king;
Escape is even yet a doubtful thing,
While to my foot these cursèd fetters cling.

Some good man 't is, within whose cart I lie,
Like cuckoo chicks, whose heartless mothers fly,
And crows must rear the fledglings, or they die. 3

I have come a long distance from the city. Shall I get out of the cart and seek a hiding-place in the grove? or shall I wait to see the owner of the cart? On second thoughts, I will not hide myself in the grove; for men say that the noble Chārudatta is ever helpful to them that seek his protection. I will not go until I have seen him face to face.

'T will bring contentment to that good man's heart
To see me rescued from misfortune's sea.
This body, in its suffering, pain, and smart,
Is saved through his sweet magnanimity. 4

*Vardhamānaka.* Here is the garden. I 'll drive in. [*He does so.*] Maitreya!

*Maitreya.* Good news, my friend. It is Vardhamānaka's voice. Vasantasenā must have come.

*Chārudatta.* Good news, indeed.

*Maitreya.* You son of a slave, what makes you so late?

*Vardhamānaka.* Don't get angry, good Maitreya. I remembered that I had forgotten the cushion, and I had to go back for it, and that is why I am late.

*Chārudatta.* Turn the cart around, Vardhamānaka. Maitreya, my friend, help Vasantasenā to get out.

*Maitreya.* Has she got fetters on her feet, so that she can't get out by herself? [*He rises and lifts the curtain of the cart.*] Why, this is n't mistress Vasantasenā—this is Mister Vasantasena.

*Chārudatta.* A truce to your jests, my friend. Love cannot wait. I will help her to get out myself. [*He rises.*]

*Aryaka.* [*Discovers him.*] Ah, the owner of the bullock-cart! He is attractive not only to the ears of men, but also to their eyes. Thank heaven! I am safe.

*Chārudatta.* [*Enters the bullock-cart and discovers Aryaka.*] Who then is this?

As trunk of elephant his arms are long,
His chest is full, his shoulders broad and strong,

His great eyes restless-red;[1]
Why should this man be thus enforced to fight—
So noble he—with such ignoble plight,
His foot to fetters wed? 5

Who are you, sir?

*Aryaka.* I am one who seeks your protection, Aryaka, by birth a herdsman.

*Chārudatta.* Are you he whom King Pālaka took from the hamlet where he lived and thrust into prison?

*Aryaka.* The same.

*Chārudatta.* 'T is fate that brings you to my sight;
May I be reft of heaven's light,
Ere I desert you in your hapless plight. 6

[*Aryaka manifests his joy.*]

*Chārudatta.* Vardhamānaka, remove the fetters from his foot.

*Vardhamānaka.* Yes, sir. [*He does so.*] Master, the fetters are removed.

*Aryaka.* But you have bound me with yet stronger fetters of love.

*Maitreya.* Now you may put on the fetters yourself. He is free anyway. And it 's time for us to be going.

*Chārudatta.* Peace! For shame!

*Aryaka.* Chārudatta, my friend, I entered your cart somewhat unceremoniously. I beg your pardon.

*Chārudatta.* I feel honored that you should use no ceremony with me.

*Aryaka.* If you permit it, I now desire to go.

*Chārudatta.* Go in peace.

*Aryaka.* Thank you. I will alight from the cart.

*Chārudatta.* No, my friend. The fetters have but this moment been removed, and you will find walking difficult. In this spot

[1] Lallādīkshita says that these are signs of royalty.

where men seek pleasure, a bullock-cart will excite no suspicion. Continue your journey then in the cart.

*Aryaka.* I thank you, sir.

*Chārud.* Seek now thy kinsmen. Happiness be thine!
*Aryaka.* Ah, I have found thee, blessèd kinsman mine!
*Chārud.* Remember me, when thou hast cause to speak.
*Aryaka.* Thy name, and not mine own, my words shall seek.
*Chārud.* May the immortal gods protect thy ways!
*Aryaka.* Thou didst protect me, in most perilous days.
*Chārud.* Nay, it was fate that sweet protection lent.
*Aryaka.* But thou wast chosen as fate's instrument. 7

*Chārudatta.* King Pālaka is aroused, and protection will prove difficult. You must depart at once.

*Aryaka.* Until we meet again, farewell. [*Exit.*

*Chārud.* From royal wrath I now have much to fear;
It were unwise for me to linger here.
Then throw the fetters in the well; for spies
Serve to their king as keen, far-seeing eyes. 8

[*His left eye twitches.*] Maitreya, my friend, I long to see Vasantasenā. For now, because

I have not seen whom I love best,
My left eye twitches; and my breast
Is causeless-anxious and distressed. 9

Come, let us go. [*He walks about.*] See! a Buddhist monk approaches, and the sight bodes ill. [*Reflecting.*] Let him enter by that path, while we depart by this. [*Exit.*

# ACT THE EIGHTH

## THE STRANGLING OF VASANTASENA

[*Enter a monk, with a wet garment in his hand.*]

*Monk.*

YE ignorant, lay by a store of virtue!
Restrain the belly; watch eternally,
Heeding the beat of contemplation's[1] drum.
For else the senses—fearful thieves they be—
Will steal away all virtue's hoarded sum. 1

And further: I have seen that all things are transitory, so that now I am become the abode of virtues alone.

Who slays the Five Men,[2] and the Female Bane,[3]
By whom protection to the Town[4] is given,
By whom the Outcaste[5] impotent is slain,
He cannot fail to enter into heaven. 2

Though head be shorn and face be shorn,
The heart unshorn, why should man shave him?
But he whose inmost heart is shorn
Needs not the shaven head to save him. 3

I have dyed this robe of mine yellow. And now I will go into the garden of the king's brother-in-law, wash it in the pond, and go away as soon as I can. [*He walks about and washes the robe.*]

*A voice behind the scenes.* Shtop, you confounded monk, shtop!

*Monk.* [*Discovers the speaker. Fearfully.*] Heaven help me! Here is the king's brother-in-law, Sansthānaka. Just because one monk committed an offense, now, wherever he sees a monk, whether it is the same one or not, he bores a hole in his nose and drives him around like a bullock. Where shall a defenseless man find a defender? But after all, the blessèd Lord Buddha is my defender.

[1] An allusion to the practice by which the Buddhists induced a state of religious ecstasy.
[2] The five senses. [3] Ignorance. [4] The body. [5] The conceit of individuality.

[*Enter the courtier, carrying a sword, and Sansthānaka.*]

*Sansthānaka.* Shtop, you confounded monk, shtop! I'll pound your head like a red radish[1] at a drinking party. [*He strikes him.*]

*Courtier.* You jackass, you should not strike a monk who wears the yellow robes of renunciation. Why heed him? Look rather upon this garden, which offers itself to pleasure.

> To creatures else forlorn, the forest trees
> Do works of mercy, granting joy and ease;
> Like a sinner's heart, the park unguarded lies,
> Like some new-founded realm, an easy prize. 4

*Monk.* Heaven bless you! Be merciful, servant of the Blessèd One!

*Sansthānaka.* Did you hear that, shir? He 's inshulting me.

*Courtier.* What does he say?

*Sansthānaka.* Shays I'm a shervant. What do you take me for? a barber?

*Courtier.* A servant of the Blessèd One he calls you, and this is praise.

*Sansthānaka.* Praise me shome more, monk!

*Monk.* You are virtuous! You are a brick!

*Sansthānaka.* Shee? He shays I 'm virtuous. He shays I 'm a brick. What do you think I am? a materialistic philosopher? or a watering-trough? or a pot-maker?[2]

*Courtier.* You jackass, he praises you when he says that you are virtuous, that you are a brick.

*Sansthānaka.* Well, shir, what did he come here for?

*Monk.* To wash this robe.

*Sansthānaka.* Confound the monk! My shishter's husband gave me the finesht garden there is, the garden Pushpakaranda. Dogs and jackals drink the water in thish pond. Now I 'm an arishtocrat, I 'm

[1] Used as an appetizer.

[2] The elaborate puns of this passage can hardly be reproduced in a translation.

a man, and I don't even take a bath. And here you bring your shtinking clothes, all shtained with shtale bean-porridge, and wash 'em! I think one good shtroke will finish you.

*Courtier.* You jackass, I am sure he has not long been a monk.

*Sansthānaka.* How can you tell, shir?

*Courtier.* It does n't take much to tell that. See!

His hair is newly shorn; the brow still white;
  The rough cloak has not yet the shoulder scarred;
He wears it awkwardly; it clings not tight;
  And here above, the fit is sadly marred.

*Monk.* True, servant of the Blessèd One. I have been a monk but a short time.

*Sansthānaka.* Then why have n't you been one all your life? [*He beats him.*]

*Monk.* Buddha be praised!

*Courtier.* Stop beating the poor fellow. Leave him alone. Let him go.

*Sansthānaka.* Jusht wait a minute, while I take counshel.

*Courtier.* With whom?

*Sansthānaka.* With my own heart.

*Courtier.* Poor fellow! Why did n't he escape?

*Sansthānaka.* Blesshèd little heart, my little shon and mashter, shall the monk go, or shall the monk shtay? [*To himself.*] Neither go, nor shtay. [*Aloud.*] Well, shir, I took counshel with my heart, and my heart shays—

*Courtier.* Says what?

*Sansthānaka.* He shall neither go, nor shtay. He shall neither breathe up, nor breathe down. He shall fall down right here and die, before you can shay "boo."

*Monk.* Buddha be praised! I throw myself upon your protection.

*Courtier.* Let him go.

*Sansthānaka.* Well, on one condition.

*Courtier.* And what is that?

*Sansthānaka.* He musht shling mud in, without making the water dirty. Or better yet, he musht make the water into a ball, and shling it into the mud.

*Courtier.* What incredible folly!

The patient earth is burdened by
So many a fool, so many a drone,
Whose thoughts and deeds are all awry—
These trees of flesh, these forms of stone. 6

[*The monk makes faces at Sansthānaka.*]

*Sansthānaka.* What does he mean?

*Courtier.* He praises you.

*Sansthānaka.* Praise me shome more! Praise me again! [*The monk does so, then exit.*]

*Courtier.* See how beautiful the garden is, you jackass.

See yonder trees, adorned with fruit and flowers,
O'er which the clinging creepers interlace;
The watchmen guard them with the royal powers;
They seem like men whom loving wives embrace. 7

*Sansthānaka.* A good deshcription, shir.

The ground is mottled with a lot of flowers;
The blosshom freight bends down the lofty trees;
And, hanging from the leafy tree-top bowers,
The monkeys bob, like breadfruit in the breeze. 8

*Courtier.* Will you be seated on this stone bench, you jackass?

*Sansthānaka.* I am sheated. [*They seat themselves.*] Do you know, shir, I remember that Vasantasenā even yet. She is like an inshult. I can't get her out of my mind.

*Courtier.* [*Aside.*] He remembers her even after such a repulse. For indeed,

The mean man, whom a woman spurns,
But loves the more;
The wise man's passion gentler burns,
Or passes o'er. 9

*Sansthānaka.* Shome time has passhed, shir, shince I told my shervant Sthāvaraka to take the bullock-cart and come as quick as he could. And even yet he is not here. I 've been hungry a long time, and at noon a man can't go a-foot. For shee!

The shun is in the middle of the shky,
And hard to look at as an angry ape;
Like Gāndhārī, whose hundred shons did die,
The earth is hard dishtresshed and can't eshcape. 10

*Courtier.* True.

The cattle all—their cuds let fall—
Lie drowsing in the shade;
In heated pool their lips to cool,
Deer throng the woodland glade;
A prey to heat, the city street
Makes wanderers afraid;
The cart must shun the midday sun,
And thus has been delayed. 11

*Sansthānaka.* Yesshir,

Fasht to my head the heated shun-beam clings;
Birds, flying creatures, alsho wingèd things
Resht in the branches of the trees, while men,
People, and pershons shigh and shigh again;
At home they tarry, in their houses shtaý,
To bear the heat and burden of the day. 12

Well, shir, that shervant is n't here yet. I 'm going to shing shomething to passh the time. [*He sings.*] There, shir, did you hear what I shang?

*Courtier.* What shall I say? Ah, how melodious!

*Sansthānaka.* Why *should n't* it be malodorous?

Of nut-grass and cumin I make up a pickle,
Of devil's-dung, ginger, and orris, and treacle;
That's the mixture of perfumes I eagerly eat:
Why should n't my voice be remarkably shweet? 13

Well, shir, I 'm jusht going to shing again. [*He does so.*] There, shir, did you hear what I shang?

*Courtier.* What shall I say? Ah, how melodious!

*Sansthānaka.* Why *should n't* it be malodorous?

Of the flesh of the cuckoo I make up a chowder,
With devil's-dung added, and black pepper powder;
With oil and with butter I shprinkle the meat:
Why should n't my voice be remarkably shweet? 14

But shir, the shervant is n't here yet.

*Courtier.* Be easy in your mind. He will be here presently.

[*Enter Vasantasenā in the bullock-cart, and Sthāvaraka.*]

*Sthāvaraka.* I 'm frightened. It is already noon. I hope Sansthānaka, the king's brother-in-law, will not be angry. I must drive faster. Get up, bullocks, get up!

*Vasantasenā.* Alas! That is not Vardhamānaka's voice. What does it mean? I wonder if Chārudatta was afraid that the bullocks might become weary, and so sent another man with another cart. My right eye twitches. My heart is all a-tremble. There is no one in sight. Everything seems to dance before my eyes.

*Sansthānaka.* [*Hearing the sound of wheels.*] The cart is here, shir.

*Courtier.* How do you know?

*Sansthānaka.* Can't you shee? It shqueaks like an old hog.

*Courtier.* [*Perceives the cart.*] Quite true. It is here.

*Sansthānaka.* Sthāvaraka, my little shon, my shlave, are you here?

*Sthāvaraka.* Yes, sir.

*Sansthānaka.* Is the cart here?

*Sthāvaraka.* Yes, sir.

*Sansthānaka.* Are the bullocks here?

*Sthāvaraka.* Yes, sir.

*Sansthānaka.* And are you here?

*Sthāvaraka.* [*Laughing.*] Yes, master, I am here too.

*Sansthānaka.* Then drive the cart in.

*Sthāvaraka.* By which road?

*Sansthānaka.* Right here, where the wall is tumbling down.

*Sthāvaraka.* Oh, master, the bullocks will be killed. The cart will go to pieces. And I, your servant, shall be killed.

*Sansthānaka.* I'm the king's brother-in-law, man. If the bullocks are killed, I'll buy shome more. If the cart goes to pieces, I'll have another one made. If you are killed, there will be another driver.

*Sthāvaraka.* Everything will be replaced—except me.

*Sansthānaka.* Let the whole thing go to pieces. Drive in over the wall.

*Sthāvaraka.* Then break, cart, break with your driver. There will be another cart. I must go and present myself to my master. [*He drives in.*] What! not broken? Master, here is your cart.

*Sansthānaka.* The bullocks not shplit in two? and the ropes not killed? and you too not killed?

*Sthāvaraka.* No, sir.

*Sansthānaka.* Come, shir. Let's look at the cart. You are my teacher, shir, my very besht teacher. You are a man I reshpect, my intimate friend, a man I delight to honor. Do you enter the cart firsht.

*Courtier.* Very well. [*He starts to do so.*]

*Sansthānaka.* Not much! Shtop! Is thish your father's cart, that you should enter it firsht? I own thish cart. I'll enter it firsht.

*Courtier.* I only did what you said.

*Sansthānaka.* Even if I do shay sho, you ought to be polite enough to shay "After you, mashter."

*Courtier.* After you, then.

*Sansthānaka.* Now I 'll enter. Sthāvaraka, my little shon, my shlave, turn the cart around.

*Sthāvaraka.* [*Does so.*] Enter, master.

*Sansthānaka.* [*Enters and looks about, then hastily gets out in terror, and falls on the courtier's neck.*] Oh, oh, oh! You're a dead man! There 's a witch, or a thief, that 's sitting and living in my bullock-cart. If it 's a witch, we 'll both be robbed. If it 's a thief, we 'll both be eaten alive.

*Courtier.* Don't be frightened. How could a witch travel in a bullock-cart? I hope that the heat of the midday sun has not blinded you, so that you became the victim of an hallucination when you saw the shadow of Sthāvaraka with the smock on it.

*Sansthānaka.* Sthāvaraka, my little shon, my shlave, are you alive?

*Sthāvaraka.* Yes, sir.

*Sansthānaka.* But shir, there 's a woman sitting and living in the bullock-cart. Look and shee!

*Courtier.* A woman?

Then let us bow our heads at once and go,
  Like steers whose eyes the falling raindrops daze;
In public spots my dignity I show;
  On high-born dames I hesitate to gaze.

*Vasantasenā.* [*In amazement. Aside.*] Oh, oh! It is that thorn in my eye, the king's brother-in-law. Alas! the danger is great. Poor woman! My coming hither proves as fruitless as the sowing of a handful of seeds on salty soil. What shall I do now?

*Sansthānaka.* Thish old shervant is afraid and he won't look into the cart. Will you look into the cart, shir?

*Courtier.* I see no harm in that. Yes, I will do it.

*Sansthānaka.* Are those things jackals that I shee flying into the air, and are those things crows that walk on all fours? While the witch is chewing him with her eyes, and looking at him with her teeth, I 'll make my eshcape.

*Courtier.* [*Perceives Vasantasenā. Sadly to himself.*] Is it possible? The gazelle follows the tiger. Alas!

Her mate is lovely as the autumn moon,
Who waits for her upon the sandy dune;
And yet the swan will leave him? and will go
To dance attendance on a common crow? 16

[*Aside to Vasantasenā.*] Ah, Vasantasenā! This is neither right, nor worthy of you.

Your pride rejected him before,
Yet now for gold, and for your mother's will

*Vasantasenā.* No! [*She shakes her head.*]

*Courtier.*

Your nature knows your pride no more;
You honor him, a common woman still. 17

Did I not tell[1] you to "serve the man you love, and him you hate"?

*Vasantasenā.* I made a mistake in the cart, and thus I came hither. I throw myself upon your protection.

*Courtier.* Do not fear. Come, I must deceive him. [*He returns to Sansthānaka.*] Jackass, there is indeed a witch who makes her home in the cart.

*Sansthānaka.* But shir, if a witch is living there, why are n't you robbed? And if it 's a thief, why are n't you eaten alive?

*Courtier.* Why try to determine that? But if we should go back on foot through the gardens until we came to the city, to Ujjayinī, what harm would that do?

*Sansthānaka.* And if we did, what then?

[1] See page 13.

*Courtier.* Then we should have some exercise, and should avoid tiring the bullocks.

*Sansthānaka.* All right. Sthāvaraka, my shlave, drive on. But no! Shtop, shtop! I go on foot before gods and Brahmans? Not much! I 'll go in my cart, sho that people shall shee me a long way off, and shay "There he goes, our mashter, the king's brother-in-law."

*Courtier.* [*Aside.*] It is hard to convert poison into medicine. So be it, then. [*Aloud.*] Jackass, this is Vasantasenā, come to visit you.

*Vasantasenā.* Heaven forbid!

*Sansthānaka.* [*Gleefully.*] Oh, oh! To visit me, an arishtocrat, a man, a regular Vāsudeva?

*Courtier.* Yes.

*Sansthānaka.* This is an unheard-of piece of luck. That other time I made her angry, sho now I 'll fall at her feet and beg her pardon.

*Courtier.* Capital!

*Sansthānaka.* I 'll fall at her feet myshelf. [*He approaches Vasantasenā.*] Little mother, mamma dear, lishten to my prayer.

I fold my hands and fall before thy feet—
Thine eyes are large, thy teeth are clean and neat,
  Thy finger-nails are ten—forgive thy shlave
What, love-tormented, he offended, shweet. 18

*Vasantasenā.* [*Angrily.*] Leave me! Your words are an insult! [*She spurns him with her foot.*]

*Sansthānaka.* [*Wrathfully.*]

Thish head that mother and that mamma kissed,
That never bent to worship god, I wist,
Upon thish head she dared to plant her feet,
Like jackals on the carrion they meet. 19

Sthāvaraka, you shlave, where did you pick her up?

*Sthāvaraka.* Master, the highway was blocked by villagers' wagons. So I stopped my cart near Chārudatta's orchard, and got out. And while I was helping a villager with his wagon, I suppose she mistook this cart for another, and climbed in.

*Sansthānaka.* Oho! she mishtook my cart for another? and did n't come to shee me? Get out of my cart, get out! You 're going to visit your poor merchant's shon, are you? Those are my bullocks you 're driving. Get out, get out, you shlave! Get out, get out!

*Vasantasenā.* Truly, you honor me when you say that I came to see Chārudatta. Now what must be, must be.

*Sansthānaka.* These hands of mine, ten-finger-naily,
These hands sho lotush-leafy,
Are itching-anxious, girl, to dally
With you; and in a jiffy
I 'll drag Your Shweetness by the hair
From the cart wherein you ride,
As did Jatāyu Bāli's fair,
The monkey Bāli's bride. 20

*Courtier.* So virtuous ladies may not be
Insulted thus despitefully;
Nor garden creepers may not be
Robbed of their leaves so cruelly. 21

Stand up, man. I will help her to alight. Come, Vasantasenā! [*Vasantasenā alights and stands apart.*]

*Sansthānaka.* [*Aside.*] The flame of wrath was kindled when she despised my proposition, and now it blazes up because she kicked me. Sho now I 'll murder her. Good! Thish way. [*Aloud.*] Well, shir, what do you want?

A cloak with fringes hanging down and all,
Tied with a hundred shtrings? or good ragout,
To make you shmack your greedy lips and call
"Chuhoo, chuhoo, chukku, chuhoo, chuhooo"? 22

*Courtier.* Well?

*Sansthānaka.* Do me a favor.

*Courtier.* Certainly. Anything, unless it be a sin.

*Sansthānaka.* There 's not a shmell of a shin in it, shir. Not a perfume!

*Courtier.* Speak, then.

*Sansthānaka.* Murder Vasantasenā.

*Courtier.* [*Stopping his ears.*]

A tender lady, gem of this our city,
A courtezan whose love was stainless ever—
If I should kill her, sinless, without pity,
What boat would bear me on the gloomy river? 23

*Sansthānaka.* I 'll give you a boat. And beshides, in thish deserted garden, who 'll shee you murdering her?

*Courtier.* The regions ten,[1] the forest gods, the sky,
The wind, the moon, the sun whose rays are light,
Virtue, my conscience—these I cannot fly,
Nor earth, that witnesses to wrong and right. 24

*Sansthānaka.* Well then, put your cloak over her and murder her.

*Courtier.* You fool! You scoundrel!

*Sansthānaka.* The old hog is afraid of a shin. Never mind. I 'll pershuade Sthāvaraka, my shlave. Sthāvaraka, my little shon, my shlave, I 'll give you golden bracelets.

*Sthāvaraka.* And I 'll wear them.

*Sansthānaka.* I 'll have a golden sheat made for you.

*Sthāvaraka.* And I 'll sit on it.

*Sansthānaka.* I 'll give you all my leavings.

*Sthāvaraka.* And I 'll eat them.

*Sansthānaka.* I 'll make you the chief of all my shervants.

*Sthāvaraka.* Master, I 'll be the chief.

*Sansthānaka.* You only have to attend to what I shay.

*Sthāvaraka.* Master, I will do anything, unless it be a sin.

[1] The four cardinal points, the four intermediate points, the zenith, and the nadir.

*Sansthānaka.* There 's not a shmell of a shin in it.

*Sthāvaraka.* Then speak, master.

*Sansthānaka.* Murder Vasantasenā.

*Sthāvaraka.* Oh, master, be merciful! Unworthy as I am, I brought this worthy lady hither, because she mistook this bullock-cart for another.

*Sansthānaka.* You shlave, ain't I your mashter?

*Sthāvaraka.* Master of my body, not of my character. Be merciful, master, be merciful! I am afraid.

*Sansthānaka.* You 're my shlave. Who are you afraid of?

*Sthāvaraka.* Of the other world, master.

*Sansthānaka.* Who is thish "other world"?

*Sthāvaraka.* Master, it is a rewarder of righteousness and sin.

*Sansthānaka.* What is the reward of righteoushness?

*Sthāvaraka.* To be like my master, with plenty of golden ornaments.

*Sansthānaka.* What is the reward of shin?

*Sthāvaraka.* To be like me, eating another man's bread. That is why I will do no sin.

*Sansthānaka.* Sho you won't murder her? [*He beats him with all his might.*]

*Sthāvaraka.* You may beat me, master. You may kill me, master. I will do no sin.

A luckless, lifelong slave am I,
A slave I live, a slave I die;
But further woe I will not buy,
I will not, will not sin.

*Vasantasenā.* Sir, I throw myself upon your protection.

*Courtier.* Pardon him, jackass! Well done, Sthāvaraka!

Does this poor, miserable slave
Seek virtue's meed beyond the grave?

And is his lord indifferent?
Then why are not such creatures sent
To instant hell, whose sinful store
Grows great, who know not virtue more? 26

And again:

Ah, cruel, cruel is our fate,
And enters through the straitest gate;
Since he is slave, and you are lord,
Since he does not enjoy your hoard,
Since you do not obey his word. 27

*Sansthānaka.* [*Aside.*] The old jackal is afraid of a shin, and the "lifelong shlave" is afraid of the other world. Who am I afraid of, I, the king's brother-in-law, an arishtocrat, a man? [*Aloud.*] Well, shervant, you "lifelong shlave," you can go. Go to your room and resht and keep out of my way.

*Sthāvaraka.* Yes, master. [*To Vasantasenā.*] Madam, I have no further power. [*Exit.*

*Sansthānaka.* [*Girds up his loins.*] Wait a minute, Vasantasenā, wait a minute. I want to murder you.

*Courtier.* You will kill her before my eyes? [*He seizes him by the throat.*]

*Sansthānaka.* [*Falls to the ground.*] Shir, you 're murdering your mashter. [*He loses consciousness, but recovers.*]

I always fed him fat with meat,
And gave him butter too, to eat;
Now for the friend in need I search;
Why does he leave me in the lurch? 28

[*After reflection.*] Good! I have an idea. The old jackal gave her a hint by shaking his head at her. Sho I 'll shend him away, and then I 'll murder Vasantasenā. That 's the idea. [*Aloud.*] Shir, I was born in a noble family as great as a wine-glass. How could I do that shin I shpoke about? I jusht shaid it to make her love me.

*Courtier.* Why should you boast of this your noble birth?
'T is character that makes the man of worth;
But thorns and weeds grow rank in fertile earth. 29

*Sansthānaka.* She 's ashamed to confessh her love when you 're here. Please go. My shervant Sthāvaraka has gone too after getting a beating. He may be running away. Catch him, shir, and come back with him.

*Courtier.* [*Aside.*]

Vasantasenā is too proud to own,
While I am near, her love for one so crude;
So now I leave her here with him alone;
Love's confidences long for solitude. 30

[*Aloud.*] Very well. I go.

*Vasantasenā.* [*Seizing the hem of his garment.*] Did I not throw myself upon your protection?

*Courtier.* Do not fear, Vasantasenā. Jackass, Vasantasenā is a pledge, committed to your hand.

*Sansthānaka.* All right. Jusht let her be committed to my hand. It 's a pledge that I 'll execute.

*Courtier.* Are you honest?

*Sansthānaka.* Honesht.

*Courtier.* [*Takes a few steps.*] No! If I go, the wretch might kill her. I will conceal myself for a moment, and see what he intends to do. [*He stands apart.*]

*Sansthānaka.* Good! I 'll murder her. But no! Perhaps thish tricky trickshter, thish Brahman, thish old jackal, has gone and hidden himshelf; he might raise a howl like the jackal he is. I 'll jusht do thish to deceive him. [*He gathers flowers and adorns himself.*] Vasantasenā, my love, my love! Come!

*Courtier.* Yes, he has turned lover. Good! I am content. I will go. [*Exit.*

*Sansthānaka.* I 'll give you gold, I 'll call you shweet;
My turbaned head adores your feet.
Why not love me, my clean-toothed girl?
Why worship such a pauper churl? 31

*Vasantasenā.* How can you ask? [*She bows her head and recites the following verses.*]

O base and vile! O wretch! What more?
Why tempt me now with gold and power?
The honey-loving bees adore
The pure and stainless lotus flower. 32

Though poverty may strike a good man low,
Peculiar honor waits upon his woe;
And 't is the glory of a courtezan
To set her love upon an honest man. 33

And I, who have loved the mango-tree, I cannot cling to the locust-tree.

*Sansthānaka.* Wench, you make that poor little Chārudatta into a mango-tree, and me you call a locusht-tree, not even an acacia! That 's the way you abuse me, and even yet you remember Chārudatta.

*Vasantasenā.* Why should I not remember him who dwells in my heart?

*Sansthānaka.* Thish very minute I 'm going to shtrangle "him who dwells in your heart," and you too. Shtand shtill, you poor-merchant-man's lover!

*Vasantasenā.* Oh speak, oh speak again these words that do me honor!

*Sansthānaka.* Jusht let poor Chārudatta—the shon of a shlave—reshcue you now!

*Vasantasenā.* He would rescue me, if he saw me.

*Sansthānaka.* Is he the king of gods? the royal ape?
Shon of a nymph? or wears a demon's shape?

The kingly deity of wind and rain?
The offshpring of the Pāndu-princes' bane?
A prophet? or a vulture known afar?
A shtatesman? or a beetle? or a shtar? 34

But even if he was, he could n't reshcue you.

As Sītā in the Bhārata
Was killed by good old Chānakya,
Sho I intend to throttle thee,
As did Jatāyu Draupadī. 35

[*He raises his arm to strike her.*]

*Vasantasenā.* Mother! where are you? Oh, Chārudatta! my heart's longing is unfulfilled, and now I die! I will scream for help. No! It would bring shame on Vasantasenā, should she scream for help. Heaven bless Chārudatta!

*Sansthānaka.* Does the wench shpeak that rashcal's name even yet? [*He seizes her by the throat.*] Remember him, wench, remember him!

*Vasantasenā.* Heaven bless Chārudatta!

*Sansthānaka.* Die, wench! [*He strangles her. Vasantasenā loses consciousness, and falls motionless.*]

*Sansthānaka.* [*Gleefully.*]

Thish bashketful of shin, thish wench,
Thish foul abode of impudence—
She came to love, she shtayed to blench,
For Death's embrace took every sense.
But why boasht I of valorous arms and shtout?
She shimply died because her breath gave out.
Like Sītā in the Bhārata, she lies.
Ah, mother mine! how prettily she dies. 36

She would not love me, though I loved the wench;
I shaw the empty garden, set the shnare,

And frightened her, and made the poor girl blench.
My brother! Oh, my father! Thish is where
You misshed the shight of heroism shtout;
Your brother and your shon here blosshomed out
Into a man; like Mother Draupadī,
You were not there, my bravery to shee. 37

Good! The old jackal will be here in a minute. I 'll shtep ashide and wait. [*He does so.*] [*Enter the courtier, with Sthāvaraka.*]

*Courtier.* I have persuaded the servant Sthāvaraka to come back, and now I will look for the jackass. [*He walks about and looks around him.*] But see! A tree has fallen by the roadside, and killed a woman in its fall. O cruel! How couldst thou do this deed of shame? And when I see that a woman was slain by thy fatal fall, I too am felled to the earth. Truly, my heart's fear for Vasantasenā was an evil omen. Oh, heaven grant that all may yet be well! [*He approaches Sansthānaka.*] Jackass, I have persuaded your servant Sthāvaraka to return.

*Sansthānaka.* How do you do, shir? Sthāvaraka, my little shon, my shlave, how do you do?

*Sthāvaraka.* Well, thank you.

*Courtier.* Give me my pledge.

*Sansthānaka.* What pledge?

*Courtier.* Vasantasenā.

*Sansthānaka.* She 's gone.

*Courtier.* Where?

*Sansthānaka.* Right after you.

*Courtier.* [*Doubtfully.*] No, she did not go in that direction.

*Sansthānaka.* In what direction did you go?

*Courtier.* Toward the east.

*Sansthānaka.* Well, she went shouth.[1]

*Courtier.* So did I.

[1] The region of Yama, god of death.

*Sansthānaka.* She went north.

*Courtier.* This is nonsense. My heart is not satisfied. Speak the truth.

*Sansthānaka.* I shwear by your head, shir, and my own feet. You may be easy in your heart. I murdered her.

*Courtier.* [*Despairingly.*] You really killed her?

*Sansthānaka.* If you don't believe my words, then shee the firsht heroic deed of Sansthānaka, the king's brother-in-law. [*He points out the body.*]

*Courtier.* Alas! Ah, woe is me! [*He falls in a swoon.*]

*Sansthānaka.* Hee, hee! The gentleman is calm enough now!

*Sthāvaraka.* Oh, sir! Come to yourself! I am the first murderer, for I brought the bullock-cart hither without looking into it.

*Courtier.* [*Comes to himself. Mournfully.*] Alas, Vasantasenā!

The stream of courtesy is dried away,
And happiness to her own land doth flee.
Sweet gem of gems, that knew love's gentle play,
Love's mart and beauty's! Joy of men like me!
Thy mirth-shored stream, that kind and healing river—
Alas! is perished, lost, and gone forever! 38

[*Tearfully.*] Ah, woe is me!

What sin is yet to come, or woe,
Now thou hast done this deed of hate?
Like sin's foul self, hast thou laid low
The sinless goddess of our state. 39

[*Aside.*] Ah! Perhaps the wretch means to lay this sin to my charge. I must go hence. [*He walks about. Sansthānaka approaches and holds him back.*] Scoundrel! Touch me not. I have done with you. I go.

*Sansthānaka.* Aha! Firsht you murder Vasantasenā, then you abuse me, and now where will you run to? And sho a man like me has n't anybody to protect him.

*Courtier.* You are an accursèd scoundrel!

*Sansth.* I 'll give you countless wealth, a piece of gold,
A copper, and a cap, to have and hold.
And sho the fame of thish great deed shall be
A common property, and shan't touch me. 40

*Courtier.* A curse upon you! Yours, and yours only, be the deed.

*Sthāvaraka.* Heaven avert the omen! [*Sansthānaka bursts out laughing.*]

*Courtier.* Be enmity between us! Cease your mirth!
Damned be a friendship that so shames my worth!
Never may I set eyes on one so low!
I fling you off, an unstrung, broken bow. 41

*Sansthānaka.* Don't be angry. Come, let 's go and play in the pond.

*Courtier.* Unstained my life, and yet it seems to me
Your friendship stains, and mocks my sinlessness.
You woman-murderer! How could I be
A friend to one whom women ever see
With eyes half-closed in apprehension's stress? 42

[*Mournfully.*] Vasantasenā,
When thou, sweet maid, art born again,
Be not a courtezan reborn,
But in a house which sinless men,
And virtuous, and good, adorn. 43

*Sansthānaka.* Firsht you murder Vasantasenā in my old garden Pushpakaranda, and now where will you run to? Come, defend yourshelf in court before my shishter's husband! [*He holds him back.*]

*Courtier.* Enough, you accursèd scoundrel! [*He draws his sword.*]

*Sansthānaka.* [*Recoiling in terror.*] Shcared, are you? Go along, then.

*Courtier.* [*Aside.*] It would be folly to remain here. Well, I will go and join myself to Sharvilaka, Chandanaka, and the rest. [*Exit.*

*Sansthānaka.* Go to hell. Well, my little shon Sthāvaraka, what kind of a thing is thish that I 've done?

*Sthāvaraka.* Master, you have committed a terrible crime.

*Sansthānaka.* Shlave! What do you mean by talking about a crime? Well, I 'll do it thish way. [*He takes various ornaments from his person.*] Take these gems. I give 'em to you. Whenever I want to wear them, I 'll take them back again, but the resht of the time they are yours.

*Sthāvaraka.* They should be worn only by my master. What have I to do with such things?

*Sansthānaka.* Go along! Take these bullocks, and wait in the tower of my palace until I come.

*Sthāvaraka.* Yes, master. [*Exit.*

*Sansthānaka.* The gentleman has made himshelf invisible. He wanted to save himshelf. And the shlave I 'll put in irons in the palace tower, and keep him there. And sho the shecret will be shafe. I 'll go along, but firsht I 'll take a look at her. Is she dead, or shall I murder her again? [*He looks at Vasantasenā.*] Dead as a doornail! Good! I 'll cover her with thish cloak. No, it has my name on it. Shome honesht man might recognize it. Well, here are shome dry leaves that the wind has blown into a heap. I 'll cover her with them. [*He does so, then pauses to reflect.*] Good! I 'll do it thish way. I 'll go to court at once, and there I 'll lodge a complaint. I 'll shay that the merchant Chārudatta enticed Vasantasenā into my old garden Pushpakaranda, and killed her for her money.

Yesh, Chārudatta musht be shlaughtered now,
  And I 'll invent the plan, forgetting pity;
The shacrificing of a sinless cow
  Is cruel in the kindesht-hearted city. 44

Now I 'm ready to go. [*He starts to go away, but perceives something that frightens him.*] Goodnessh gracioush me! Wherever I go, thish damned monk comes with his yellow robes. I bored a hole in his nose once and drove him around, and he hates me. Perhaps he 'll shee me, and will tell people that I murdered her. How shall I eshcape? [*He looks about.*] Aha! I 'll jump over the wall where it is half fallen down, and eshcape that way.

I run, I run, I go,
In heaven, on earth below,
  In hell, and in Ceylon,
  Hanūmat's peaks upon—
Like Indra's self, I go. [*Exit.*] 45

[*Enter hurriedly the Buddhist monk, ex-shampooer.*]

*Monk.* I 've washed these rags of mine. Shall I let them dry on a branch? no, the monkeys would steal them. On the ground? the dust would make them dirty again. Well then, where shall I spread them out to dry? [*He looks about.*] Ah, here is a pile of dry leaves which the wind has blown into a heap. I 'll spread them out on that. [*He does so.*] Buddha be praised! [*He sits down.*] Now I will repeat a hymn of the faith.

Who slays the Five Men, and the Female Bane,
  By whom protection to the Town is given,
By whom the Outcaste impotent is slain,
  He cannot fail to enter into heaven. (2)

After all, what have I to do with heaven, before I have paid my debt to Vasantasenā, my sister in Buddha? She bought my freedom for ten gold-pieces from the gamblers, and since that day I regard myself as her property. [*He looks about.*] What was that? a sigh that arose from the leaves? It cannot be.

The heated breezes heat the leaves,
The wetted garment wets the leaves,
And so, I guess, the scattered leaves
Curl up like any other leaves. 46

[*Vasantasenā begins to recover consciousness, and stretches out her hand.*]

*Monk.* Ah, there appears a woman's hand, adorned with beautiful gems. What! a second hand? [*He examines it with the greatest care.*] It seems to me, I recognize this hand. Yes, there is no doubt about it. Surely, this is the hand that saved me. But I must see for myself. [*He uncovers the body, looks at it, and recognizes it.*] It *is* my sister in Buddha. [*Vasantasenā pants for water.*] Ah, she seeks water, and the pond is far away. What shall I do? An idea! I will hold this robe over her and let it drip upon her. [*He does so. Vasantasenā recovers consciousness, and raises herself. The monk fans her with his garment.*]

*Vasantasenā.* Who are you, sir?

*Monk.* Has my sister in Buddha forgotten him whose freedom she bought for ten gold-pieces?

*Vasantasenā.* I seem to remember, but not just as you say. It were better that I had slept never to waken.

*Monk.* What happened here, sister in Buddha?

*Vasantasenā.* [*Despairingly.*] Nothing but what is fitting—for a courtezan.

*Monk.* Sister in Buddha, support yourself by this creeper[1] that clings to the tree, and rise to your feet. [*He bends down the creeper. Vasantasenā takes it in her hand, and rises.*]

*Monk.* In yonder monastery dwells one who is my sister in the faith. There shall my sister in Buddha be restored before she returns home. You must walk very slowly, sister. [*He walks about and looks around him.*] Make way, good people, make way! This is a young lady, and I am a monk, yet my conduct is above reproach.

The man whose hands, whose lips are free from greed,
Who curbs his senses, he is man indeed.
He little recks, if kingdoms fall or stand;
For heaven is in the hollow of his hand. 47

[*Exeunt.*

[1] A monk may not touch a woman.

## ACT THE NINTH

### THE TRIAL

[*Enter a beadle.*]

*Beadle.* THE magistrates said to me "Come, beadle, go to the court-room, and make ready the seats." So now I am on my way to set the court-room in order. [*He walks about and looks around him.*] Here is the court-room. I will enter. [*He enters, sweeps, and puts a seat in its place.*] There! I have tidied up the court-room and put the seats in readiness, and now I will go and tell the magistrates. [*He walks about and looks around him.*] But see! Here comes that arrant knave, the king's brother-in-law. I will go away without attracting his attention. [*He stands apart. Enter Sansthānaka, in gorgeous raiment.*]

*Sansth.* I bathed where water runs and flows and purls;
I shat within a garden, park, and grove
With women, and with females, and with girls,
Whose lovely limbs with grace angelic move. 1

My hair is shometimes done up tight, you shee;
In locks, or curls, it hangs my forehead o'er;
Shometimes 't is matted, shometimes hanging free;
And then again, I wear a pompadour.
I am a wonder, I 'm a wondrous thing,
And the husband of my shishter is the king. 2

And beshides, I 've found a big hole, like a worm that has crawled into the knot of a lotush-root, and is looking for a hole to creep out at. Now who was I going to accuse of thish wicked deed? [*He recalls something.*] Oh, yesh! I remember. I was going to accuse poor Chārudatta of thish wicked deed. Beshides, he 's poor. They 'll believe anything about him. Good! I 'll go to the court-room and lodge a public complaint against Chārudatta, how he shtrangled

Vasantasenā and murdered her. Sho now I'm on my way to the court-room. [*He walks about and looks around him.*] Here is the court-room. I'll go in. [*He enters and looks about.*] Well, here are the sheats, all arranged. While I'm waiting for the magishtrates, I'll jusht sit down a minute on the grass. [*He does so.*]

*Beadle.* [*Walks about in another direction, and looks before him.*] Here come the magistrates. I will go to them. [*He does so.*]

[*Enter the judge, accompanied by a gild-warden, a clerk, and others.*]

*Judge.* Gild-warden and clerk!

*Gild-warden and Clerk.* We await your bidding.

*Judge.* A trial depends to such an extent upon others that the task of the magistrates—the reading of another's thoughts—is most difficult.

Men often speak of deeds that no man saw,
Matters beyond the province of the law;
Passion so rules the parties that their lies
Hide their offenses from judicial eyes;
This side and that exaggerate a thing,
Until at last it implicates the king;
To sum it up: false blame is easy won,
A true judge little praised, or praised by none. 3

And again:

Men often point to sins that no man saw,
And in their anger scorn the patient law;
In court-rooms even the righteous with their lies
Hide their offenses from judicial eyes;
And those who did the deed are lost to view,
Who sinned with plaintiff and defendant too;
To sum it up: false blame is easy won,
A true judge little praised, or praised by none. 4

For the judge must be

Learnèd, and skilled in tracing fraud's sly path,
And eloquent, insensible to wrath;

To friend, foe, kinsman showing equal grace,
Reserving judgment till he know the case;
Untouched by avarice, in virtue sound,
The weak he must defend, the knave confound;
An open door to truth, his heart must cling
To others' interests, yet shun each thing
That might awake the anger of the king.

*Gild-warden and Clerk.* And do men speak of defects in your virtue? If so, then they speak of darkness in the moonlight.

*Judge.* My good beadle, conduct me to the court-room.

*Beadle.* Follow me, Your Honor. [*They walk about.*] Here is the court-room. May the magistrates be pleased to enter. [*All enter.*]

*Judge.* My good beadle, do you go outside and learn who desires to present a case.

*Beadle.* Yes, sir. [*He goes out.*] Gentlemen, the magistrates ask if there is any here who desires to present a case.

*Sansthānaka.* [*Gleefully.*] The magishtrates are here. [*He struts about.*] I desire to present a cashe, I, an arishtocrat, a man, a Vāsudeva, the royal brother-in-law, the brother-in-law of the king.

*Beadle.* [*In alarm.*] Goodness! The king's brother-in-law is the first who desires to present a case. Well! Wait a moment, sir. I will inform the magistrates at once. [*He approaches the magistrates.*] Gentlemen, here is the king's brother-in-law who has come to court, desiring to present a case.

*Judge.* What! the king's brother-in-law is the first who desires to present a case? Like an eclipse at sunrise, this betokens the ruin of some great man. Beadle, the court will doubtless be very busy to-day. Go forth, my good man, and say "Leave us for to-day. Your suit cannot be considered."

*Beadle.* Yes, Your Honor. [*He goes out, and approaches Sansthānaka.*] Sir, the magistrates send word that you are to leave them for to-day; that your suit cannot be considered.

*Sansthānaka.* [*Wrathfully.*] Confound it! Why can't my shuit be conshidered? If it is n't conshidered, then I 'll tell my brother-in-law, King Pālaka, my shishter's husband, and I 'll tell my shishter and my mother too, and I 'll have thish judge removed, and another judge appointed. [*He starts to go away.*]

*Beadle.* Oh, sir! Brother-in-law of the king! Wait a moment. I will inform the magistrates at once. [*He returns to the judge.*] The brother-in-law of the king is angry, and says—[*He repeats Sansthānaka's words.*]

*Judge.* This fool might do anything. My good man, tell him to come hither, that his suit will be considered.

*Beadle.* [*Approaching Sansthānaka.*] Sir, the magistrates send word that you are to come in, that your suit will be considered. Pray enter, sir.

*Sansthānaka.* Firsht they shay it won't be conshidered, then they shay it will be conshidered. The magishtrates are shcared. Whatever I shay, I 'll make 'em believe it. Good! I 'll enter. [*He enters and approaches the magistrates.*] I am feeling very well, thank you. Whether you feel well or not—that depends on me.

*Judge.* [*Aside.*] Well, well! We seem to have a highly cultivated plaintiff. [*Aloud.*] Pray be seated.

*Sansthānaka.* Well! Thish floor belongs to me. I 'll sit down wherever I like. [*To the gild-warden.*] I 'll sit here. [*To the beadle.*] Why should n't I sit here? [*He lays his hand on the judge's head.*] I 'll sit here. [*He sits down on the floor.*]

*Judge.* You desire to present a case?

*Sansthānaka.* Of courshe.

*Judge.* Then state the case.

*Sansthānaka.* I 'll whishper it. I was born in the great family of a man as glorioush as a wine-glass.

My father 's father of the king—in law;  
The king, he is my daddy's son-in-law;

And I am brother to the king—in law;
And the husband of my shishter is the king. 6

*Judge.* All this we know.

Why should you boast of this your noble birth?
'T is character that makes the man of worth;
But thorns and weeds grow rank in fertile earth. 7

State your case.

*Sansthānaka.* I will, but even if I was guilty, he would n't do anything to me. Well, my shishter's husband liked me, and gave me the besht garden there is, the old garden Pushpakaranda, to play in and look after. And there I go every day to look at it, to keep it dry, to keep it clean, to keep it blosshoming, to keep it trimmed. But fate decreed that I shaw—or rather, I did n't *shee*—the proshtrate body of a woman.

*Judge.* Do you know who the unfortunate woman was?

*Sansthānaka.* Hello, magishtrates! Why should n't I know? A woman like that! the pearl of the city! adorned with a hundred golden ornaments! Shomebody's unworthy shon enticed her into the old garden Pushpakaranda when it was empty, and for a mere trifle—for her money!—shtrangled Vasantasenā and killed her. But *I* did n't—[*He breaks off, and puts his hand over his mouth.*]

*Judge.* What carelessness on the part of the city police! Gildwarden and clerk, write down the words "I did n't," as the first article in the case.

*Clerk.* Yes, sir. [*He does so.*] Sir, it is written.

*Sansthānaka.* [*Aside.*] Goodnessh! Now I 've ruined myshelf, like a man that shwallows a cake of rice and milk in a hurry. Well, I 'll get out of it thish way. [*Aloud.*] Well, well, magishtrates! I was jusht remarking that I did n't shee it happen. What are you making thish hullabaloo about? [*He wipes out the written words with his foot.*]

*Judge.* How do you know that she was strangled—and for her money?

*Sansthānaka.* Hello! Why should n't I think sho, when her neck was shwollen and bare, and the places where you wear jewels did n't have any gold on them?

*Gild-warden and Clerk.* That seems plausible.

*Sansthānaka.* [*Aside.*] Thank heaven! I breathe again. Hooray!

*Gild-warden and Clerk.* Upon whom does the conduct of this case depend?

*Judge.* The case has a twofold aspect.

*Gild-warden and Clerk.* How so?

*Judge.* We have to consider the allegations, then the facts. Now the investigation of the allegations depends upon plaintiff and defendant. But the investigation of the facts must be carried out by the wisdom of the judge.

*Gild-warden and Clerk.* Then the conduct of the case depends upon the presence of Vasantasenā's mother?

*Judge.* Precisely. My good beadle, summon Vasantasenā's mother, without, however, giving her cause for anxiety.

*Beadle.* Yes, Your Honor. [*He goes out, and returns with the mother of the courtezan.*] Follow me, madam.

*Mother.* My daughter went to the house of a friend to enjoy her youth. But now comes this gentleman—long life to him!—and says "Come! The judge summons you." I find myself quite bewildered. My heart is palpitating. Sir, will you conduct me to the court-room?

*Beadle.* Follow me, madam. [*They walk about.*] Here is the court-room. Pray enter, madam. [*They enter.*]

*Mother.* [*Approaching.*] Happiness be yours, most worthy gentlemen.

*Judge.* My good woman, you are very welcome. Pray be seated.

*Mother*. Thank you. [*She seats herself.*]

*Sansthānaka*. [*Abusively.*] You 're here, are you, you old bawd?

*Judge*. Tell me. Are you Vasantasenā's mother?

*Mother*. I am.

*Judge*. Whither has Vasantasenā gone at this moment?

*Mother*. To the house of a friend.

*Judge*. What is the name of her friend?

*Mother*. [*Aside.*] Dear me! Really, this is very embarrassing. [*Aloud.*] Any one else might ask me this, but not a judge.

*Judge*. Pray do not be embarrassed. The conduct of the case puts the question.

*Gild-warden and Clerk*. The conduct of the case puts the question. You incur no fault. Speak.

*Mother*. What! the conduct of the case? If that is so, then listen, worthy gentlemen. There lives in the merchants' quarter the grandson of the merchant Vinayadatta, the son of Sāgaradatta, a man whose name is a good omen in itself—that name is Chārudatta. In his house my daughter enjoys her youth.

*Sansthānaka*. Did you hear that? Write those words down. My contention is with Chārudatta.

*Gild-warden and Clerk*. It is no sin for Chārudatta to be her friend.

*Judge*. The conduct of this case demands the presence of Chārudatta.

*Gild-warden and Clerk*. Exactly.

*Judge*. Dhanadatta, write as the first article in the case "Vasantasenā went to the house of Chārudatta." But must we summon the worthy Chārudatta also? No, the conduct of the case summons him. Go, my good beadle, summon Chārudatta,—but gently, without haste, without giving him cause for anxiety, respectfully, as it were incidentally,—with the words "The judge wishes to see you."

*Beadle.* Yes, Your Honor. [*He goes out, then returns with Chārudatta.*] Follow me, sir.

*Chārudatta.* [*Thoughtfully.*]

My character and kin are known
Unto the king who rules our state;
And in this summons there is shown
A doubt begotten of my wretched fate. 8

[*Reflectively. Aside.*]

Ah! Were there those, the man to recognize
Who met me on the road, from bondage freed?
Or did the king, who sees through cunning spies,
Learn that my cart was lent him in his need?
Why should I else be forced to tread the street,
Like one accused of crime, my judge to meet? 9

But why consider thus? I must go to the court-room. My good beadle, conduct me to the court.

*Beadle.* Follow me, sir. [*They walk about.*]

*Chārudatta.* [*Apprehensively.*] And what means this?

Hear how the gloomy raven hoarsely croaks;
The slaves of justice summon me again;
My left eye twitches; these repeated strokes
Of threatened evil frighten me and pain. 10

*Beadle.* Follow me, sir, gently and without haste.

*Chārudatta.* [*Walks about and looks before him.*]

Upon the withered tree, a crow
Turns to the sun;
His left eye falls on me. Ah, woe!
My doubt is done. 11

[*He looks in another direction.*] But see! a snake!

His eye is fixed upon me; and his back
Flashes like antimony's lustrous black;

His long tongue quivers; four white fangs appear;
His belly swells and coils. He slumbered here,
This prince of serpents, till I crossed his path,
And now he darts upon me in his wrath. 12

And more than this:

I slip, although the ground has felt no rain;
My left eye, and my left arm throb again;
Another bird is screaming overhead;
All bodes a cruel death, and hope is fled. 13

Surely, the gods will grant that all may yet be well.

*Beadle.* Follow me, sir. Here is the court-room. Pray enter.

*Chārudatta.* [*Enters and looks about.*] How wonderfully splendid is the court-room. For it seems an ocean,

Whose waters are the king's advisers, deep
In thought; as waves and shells it seems to keep
The attorneys; and as sharks and crocodiles
It has its spies that stand in waiting files;
Its elephants and horses[1] represent
The cruel ocean-fish on murder bent;
As if with herons of the sea, it shines
With screaming pettifoggers' numerous lines;
While in the guise of serpents, scribes are creeping
  Upon its statecraft-trodden shore: the court
The likeness of an ocean still is keeping,
  To which all harmful-cruel beasts resort. 14

Come! [*As he enters, he strikes his head against the door. Reflectively.*] Alas! This also?

My left eye throbs; a raven cries;
  A serpent coils athwart my path.
My safety now with heaven lies. 15

But I must enter. [*He does so.*]

[1] Elephants were employed as executioners; and, according to Lallādīkshita, the horses served the same purpose.

*Judge*. This is Chārudatta.

A countenance like his, with clear-cut nose,
Whose great, wide-opened eye frank candor shows,
Is not the home of wantonness;
With elephants, with horses, and with kine,
The outer form is inner habit's sign;
With men no less. 16

*Chārudatta*. My greetings to the officers of justice. Officials, I salute you.

*Judge*. [*Betraying his agitation.*] You are very welcome, sir. My good beadle, give the gentleman a seat.

*Beadle*. [*Brings a seat.*] Here is a seat. Pray be seated, sir. [*Chārudatta seats himself.*]

*Sansthānaka*. [*Angrily.*] You 're here, are you, you woman-murderer? Well! Thish is a fine trial, thish is a jusht trial, where they give a sheat to thish woman-murderer. [*Haughtily.*] But it 's all right. They can give it to him.

*Judge*. Chārudatta, have you any attachment, or affection, or friendship, with this lady's daughter?

*Chārudatta*. What lady?

*Judge*. This lady. [*He indicates Vasantasenā's mother.*]

*Chārudatta*. [*Rising.*] Madam, I salute you.

*Mother*. Long life to you, my son! [*Aside.*] So this is Chārudatta. My daughter's youth is in good hands.

*Judge*. Sir, is the courtezan your friend? [*Chārudatta betrays his embarrassment.*]

*Sansthānaka*. He tries to hide the deed he did;
He lies, from shame or fear;
He murdered her, of her got rid
For gold, and thinks the deed is hid;
Not sho his mashter here. 17

*Gild-warden and Clerk.* Speak, Chārudatta. Do not be ashamed. This is a lawsuit.

*Chārudatta.* [*In embarrassment.*] Officials, how can I testify that a courtezan is my friend? But at worst, it is youth that bears the blame, not character.

*Judge.*
The case is hard; then banish shame,
Though it oppress your heart;
Speak truth with fortitude, and aim
To set deceit apart. 18

Do not be embarrassed. The conduct of the case puts the question.

*Chārudatta.* Officer, with whom have I a lawsuit?

*Sansthānaka.* [*Arrogantly.*] With me!

*Chārudatta.* A lawsuit with you is unendurable!

*Sansthānaka.* Well, well, woman-murderer! You murder a woman like Vasantasenā who used to wear a hundred gems, and now you try deceitful deceivings to hide it!

*Chārudatta.* You are a fool.

*Judge.* Enough of him, good Chārudatta. Speak the truth. Is the courtezan your friend?

*Chārudatta.* She is.

*Judge.* Sir, where is Vasantasenā?

*Chārudatta.* She has gone home.

*Gild-warden and Clerk.* How did she go? When did she go? Who accompanied her?

*Chārudatta.* [*Aside.*] Shall I say that she went unobserved?

*Gild-warden and Clerk.* Speak, sir.

*Chārudatta.* She went home. What more shall I say?

*Sansthānaka.* She was enticed into my old garden Pushpakaranda, and was shtrangled for her money. Now will you shay that she went home?

*Chārudatta.* Man, you are crazy.

The very clouds of heaven wet not you;
  Your lips are like the blue-jay's wing-tip worn,
Yes, full as fickle with their speech untrue,
  And like the winter lotus lustre-lorn. 19

*Judge.* [*Aside.*]

Take the Himalayan hills within your hand,
And swim from ocean strand to ocean strand,
And hold within your grasp the fleeting wind:
Then may you think that Chārudatta sinned. 20

[*Aloud.*] This is the noble Chārudatta. How could he commit this crime? [*He repeats the verse* "A countenance like his:" *page 141.*]

*Sansthānaka.* Why thish partiality in a lawshuit?

*Judge.* Away, you fool!

Illiterate, you gloss the Sacred Law,
  And still your tongue uninjured find?
The midday sun with steadfast eye you saw,
  And are not straightway stricken blind?
You thrust your hand into the blazing fire,
  And draw it forth, unscathed and sound?
Drag Chārudatta's virtue in the mire,
  Nor sink beneath this yawning ground? 21

How could the noble Chārudatta commit a crime?

Of all the riches of the mighty sea
  Only the swelling waters now are left,
Because, without consideration, he—
  For others' good—himself of all has reft.
And should this high-souled man, this store-house where
  All gems of virtue gather and unite,
For lucre's sake, so foul a trespass dare
  That in it even his foe could not delight? 22

*Mother.* You scoundrel! When the golden casket that was left with him as a pledge was stolen by thieves at night, he gave in place of it a pearl necklace that was the pride of the four seas. And he should now, for a mere trifle—for her money!—do this sin? Oh, my child, come back to me, my daughter! [*She weeps.*]

*Judge.* Noble Chārudatta, did she go on foot, or in a bullock-cart?

*Chārudatta.* I did not see her when she went. Therefore I do not know whether she went on foot, or in a bullock-cart.

[*Enter Vīraka, in anger.*]

*Vīraka.* My anger was so prodded to the quick
By that dishonoring, insulting kick,
And so I brooded, till at last the night
Unwilling yielded to the dawning light. 23

So now I will go to the court-room. [*He enters.*] May happiness be the lot of these honorable gentlemen.

*Judge.* Ah, it is Vīraka, the captain of the guard. Vīraka, what is the purpose of your coming?

*Vīraka.* Well! I was looking for Aryaka, in all the excitement about his escape from prison. I had my suspicions about a covered bullock-cart that was coming, and wanted to look in. "You 've made one inspection, man, I must make another," said I, and then I was kicked by the highly respectable Chandanaka. You have heard the matter, gentlemen. The rest is your affair.

*Judge.* My good man, do you know to whom the bullock-cart belonged?

*Vīraka.* To this gentleman here, Chārudatta. And the driver said that Vasantasenā was in it, and was on her way to have a good time in the old garden Pushpakaranda.

*Sansthānaka.* Lishten to that, too!

*Judge.* This moon, alas, though spotless-bright,
Is now eclipsed, and robbed of light;

The bank is fallen; the waves appear
Befouled, that once were bright and clear. 24

Vīraka, we will investigate your case here later. Mount the horse that stands before the court-room door, go to the garden Pushpakaranda, and see whether a woman has perished there or not.

*Vīraka.* Yes, sir. [*He goes out, then returns.*] I have been there. And I saw the body of a woman, torn by wild beasts.

*Gild-warden and Clerk.* How do you know that it was the body of a woman?

*Vīraka.* That I perceived from the traces of hair and arms and hands and feet.

*Judge.* Alas for the difficulties which are caused by the actions of men!

The more one may apply his skill,
The harder is the matter still;
Plain are indeed the law's demands,
Yet judgment insecurely stands
As some poor cow on shifting sands. 25

*Chārudatta.* [*Aside.*]

As bees, when flowers begin to blow,
Gather to sip the honey, so
When man is marked by adverse fate,
Misfortunes enter every gate. 26

*Judge.* Noble Chārudatta, speak truth!

*Chārudatta.* A mean and jealous creature, passion-blind,
Sets all his soul, some fatal means to find
To slay the man he envies; shall his lies
By evil nature prompted, win the prize?
No! he is unregarded by the wise. 27

And more than this:

The creeper's beauty would I never blight,
Nor pluck its flowers; should I not be afraid

To seize her hair so lovely-long, and bright
  As wings of bees, and slay a weeping maid? 28

*Sansthānaka.* Hello, magishtrates! How can you inveshtigate the cashe with such partiality? Why, even now you let thish shcoundrel Chārudatta shtay on his sheat.

*Judge.* My good beadle, so be it. [*The beadle follows Sansthānaka's suggestion.*]

*Chārudatta.* Consider, magistrates, consider what you are doing! [*He leaves his seat, and sits on the floor.*]

*Sansthānaka.* [*Dancing about gleefully. Aside.*] Fine! The shin that I did falls on another man's head. Sho I 'll sit where Chārudatta was. [*He does so.*] Look at me, Chārudatta, and confessh that you murdered her.

*Chārudatta.* Magistrates!

A mean and jealous creature, passion-blind,
Sets all his soul, some fatal means to find
To slay the man he envies; shall his lies,
By evil nature prompted, win the prize?
No! he is unregarded by the wise. (27)

[*Sighing. Aside.*]

My friend Maitreya! Oh, this cruel blow!
  My wife, thou issue of a spotless strain!
My Rohasena! Here am I, laid low
By sternest fate; and thou, thou dost not know
  That all thy childish games are played in vain.
  Thou playest, heedless of another's pain! 29

But Maitreya I sent to Vasantasenā, that he might bring me tidings of her, and might restore the jewels which she gave my child, to buy him a toy cart. Why then does he linger?

[*Enter Maitreya with the gems.*]

*Maitreya.* Chārudatta bade me go to Vasantasenā, to return her jewels, and he said to me: "Maitreya, Vasantasenā adorned my dear Rohasena with her own jewels, and sent him thus to his mother. It was fitting that she should give him the jewels, but not that we should receive them. Therefore restore them to her." So now I will go to Vasantasenā's house. [*He walks about and looks around, then speaks to a person behind the scenes.*] Ah, it is Master Rebhila. Oh, Master Rebhila, why do you seem so exceedingly troubled? [*He listens.*] What! do you mean to say that my dear friend Chārudatta has been summoned to court? That can hardly be an insignificant matter. [*He reflects.*] I will go to Vasantasenā's house later, but now I will go to the court-room. [*He walks about and looks around.*] Here is the court-room. I will go in at once. [*He enters.*] May happiness be the lot of the magistrates. Where is my friend?

*Judge.* Here.

*Maitreya.* My friend, I wish you happiness.

*Chārudatta.* It will be mine.

*Maitreya.* And peace.

*Chārudatta.* That too will be mine.

*Maitreya.* My friend, why do you seem so exceedingly troubled? And why were you summoned?

*Chārudatta.* My friend,

A scoundrel I, who bear the blame,
Nor seek in heaven to be blest;
A maid—or goddess—'t is the same—
But *he* will say the rest.

*Maitreya.* What? what?

*Chārudatta.* [*Whispers.*] That is it.

*Maitreya.* Who says that?

*Chārudatta.* [*Indicating Sansthānaka.*] This poor fellow is the instrument that fate uses to accuse me.

*Maitreya.* [*Aside to Chārudatta.*] Why don't you simply say that she went home?

*Chārudatta.* Though I say it, it is not believed, so unfortunate is my condition.

*Maitreya.* But gentlemen! He adorned the city of Ujjayinī with mansions, cloisters, parks, temples, pools, and fountains, and he should be mad enough to commit such a crime—and for a mere trifle? [*Wrathfully.*] You offspring of a loose wench, you brother-in-law of the king, Sansthānaka, you libertine, you slanderer, you buffoon, you gilded monkey, say it before me! This friend of mine does n't even draw a flowering jasmine creeper to himself, to gather the blossoms, for fear that a twig might perhaps be injured. How should he commit a crime like this, which heaven and earth call accursèd? Just wait, you son of a bawd! Wait till I split your head into a hundred pieces with this staff of mine, as crooked as your heart.

*Sansthānaka.* [*Angrily.*] Lishten to that, gentlemen! I have a quarrel, or a lawshuit, with Chārudatta. What right has a man with a pate that looks like a caret, to shplit my head into a hundred pieces? Not much! You confounded rashcal! [*Maitreya raises his staff and repeats his words. Sansthānaka rises angrily and strikes him. Maitreya strikes back. During the scuffle the jewels fall from Maitreya's girdle.*]

*Sansthānaka.* [*Picks up the jewels and examines them. Excitedly.*] Look, gentlemen, look! These are the poor girl's jewels! [*Pointing to Chārudatta.*] For a trifle like thish he murdered her, and killed her too. [*The magistrates all bow their heads.*]

*Chārudatta.* [*Aside to Maitreya.*]

'T is thus my fate would vent its gall,
That at this moment they should fall,
These gems—and with them, I. 31

*Maitreya.* But why don't you simply tell the truth?

*Chārudatta.* My friend,

The king perceives with blinded eye,
Nor on the truth that eye will bend;
Though telling all, I cannot fly
A wretched and inglorious end. 32

*Judge.* Alas! Alas!

With Mars strives Jupiter, and dies;
Beside them both there seems to rise
A comet-planet[1] in the skies. 33

*Gild-warden and Clerk.* [*Looking at the casket. To Vasantasenā's mother.*] Madam, pray examine this golden casket attentively, to see whether it be the same or not.

*Mother.* [*Examining the casket.*] It is similar, but not the same.

*Sansthānaka.* Oh, you old bawd! You confessh it with your eyes, and deny it with your lips.

*Mother.* Away, you scoundrel!

*Gild-warden and Clerk.* Speak carefully. Is it the same or not?

*Mother.* Sir, the craftsman's skill captivates the eye. But it is not the same.

*Judge.* My good woman, do you know these jewels?

*Mother.* No, I said. No! I don't recognize them; but perhaps they were made by the same craftsman.

*Judge.* Gild-warden, see!

Gems often seem alike in many ways,
When the artist's mind on form and beauty plays;
For craftsmen imitate what they have seen,
And skilful hands remake what once has been. 34

*Gild-warden and Clerk.* Do these jewels belong to Chārudatta?

*Chārudatta.* Never!

*Gild-warden and Clerk.* To whom then?

[1] This refers to the fallen jewels.

*Chārudatta.* To this lady's daughter.

*Gild-warden and Clerk.* How did she lose them?

*Chārudatta.* She lost them. Yes, so much is true.

*Gild-warden and Clerk.* Chārudatta, speak the truth in this matter. For you must remember,

Truth brings well-being in its train;
  Through speaking truth, no evils rise;
Truth, precious syllable!—Refrain
  From hiding truth in lies. 35

*Chārudatta.* The jewels, the jewels! I do not know. But I do know that they were taken from my house.

*Sansthānaka.* Firsht you take her into the garden and murder her. And now you hide it by tricky trickinessh.

*Judge.* Noble Chārudatta, speak the truth!

Merciless lashes wait to smite
  This moment on thy tender flesh;
And we—we can but think it right. 36

*Chārudatta.* Of sinless sires I boast my birth,
  And sin in me was never found;
Yet if suspicion taints my worth,
  What boots it though my heart be sound? 37

[*Aside.*] And yet I know not what to do with life, so I be robbed of Vasantasenā. [*Aloud.*] Ah, why waste words?

A scoundrel I, who bear the blame,
  Nor think of earth, nor heaven blest;
That sweetest maid, in passion's flame—
  But *he* will say the rest. 38

*Sansthānaka.* Killed her! Come, you shay it too. "I killed her."

*Chārudatta.* You have said it.

*Sansthānaka.* Lishten, my mashters, lishten! He murdered her! No one but him! Doubt is over. Let punishment be inflicted on the body of thish poor Chārudatta.

*Judge.* Beadle, we must do as the king's brother-in-law says. Guardsmen, lay hold on this Chārudatta. [*The guardsmen do so.*]

*Mother.* Be merciful, good gentlemen, be merciful! [*She repeats what she had said before, beginning* "When the golden casket:" *page 143.*] If my daughter is killed, she is killed. Let him live for me — bless him! And besides, a lawsuit is a matter between plaintiff and defendant. I am the real plaintiff. So let him go free!

*Sansthānaka.* You shlave, get out of the way! What have you got to shay about him?

*Judge.* Go, madam. Guardsmen, conduct her forth.

*Mother.* Oh, my child, my son! [*Exit weeping.*

*Sansthānaka.* [*Aside.*] I've done shomething worthy of myshelf. Now I'll go. [*Exit.*

*Judge.* Noble Chārudatta, the decision lies with us, but the rest depends on the king. And yet, beadle, let King Pālaka be reminded of this:

> The Brahman who has sinned, our laws declare,
> May not be slain, but banished from the realm,
> And with his wealth entire abroad may fare. 39

*Beadle.* Yes, Your Honor. [*He goes out, then reënters in tears.*] Oh, sirs, I was with the king. And King Pālaka says: "Inasmuch as he killed Vasantasenā for such a trifle, these same jewels shall be hung about his neck, the drum shall be beaten, he shall be conducted to the southern burying-ground, and there impaled." And whoever else shall commit such a crime, shall be punished with the like dreadful doom.

*Chārudatta.* Oh, how wanton is this act of King Pālaka! Nevertheless,

> Although his counsellors may plunge a king
> Into injustice' dangers great,
> Yet he will reap the woe and suffering;
> And 't is a righteous fate. 40

And more than this:

They who pervert the king's true bent,
  The white crow's part who play,
Have slain their thousands innocent,
  And slay, and slay, and slay. 41

My friend Maitreya, go, greet the mother of my son in my name for the last time. And keep my son Rohasena free from harm.

*Maitreya.* When the root is cut away, how can the tree be saved?

*Chārudatta.* No, not so.

When man departs to worlds above,
  In living son yet liveth he;
Bestow on Rohasena love
  No less than that thou gavest me. 42

*Maitreya.* Oh, my friend! I will prove myself your friend by continuing the life that you leave unfinished.

*Chārudatta.* And let me see Rohasena for a single moment.

*Maitreya.* I will. It is but fitting.

*Judge.* My good beadle, remove this man. [*The beadle does so.*] Who is there? Let the headsmen receive their orders. [*The guardsmen loose their hold on Chārudatta, and all of them go out.*]

*Beadle.* Come with me, sir.

*Chārudatta.* [*Mournfully repeats the verse, page 146, beginning* "My friend Maitreya!" *Then, as if speaking to one not present.*]

If you had proved my conduct by the fire,
  By water, poison, scales, and thus had known
  That I deserved that saws should bite my bone,
My Brahman's frame, more could I not desire.
  You trust a foeman, slay me thus? 'T is well.
  With sons, and sons' sons, now you plunge to hell! 43

I come! I come! [*Exeunt omnes.*

## ACT THE TENTH

### THE END

[*Enter Chārudatta, accompanied by two headsmen.*]

*Headsmen.* THEN think no longer of the pain;
In just a second you 'll be slain.
We understand the fashions new
To fetter you and kill you too.
In chopping heads we never fail,
Nor when the victim we impale. 1

Out of the way, gentlemen, out of the way! This is the noble Chārudatta.

The oleander on his brow,
In headsmen's hands you see him now;
Like a lamp whose oil runs nearly dry,
His light fades gently, ere it die. 2

*Chārudatta.* [*Gloomily.*]

My body wet by tear-drops falling, falling;
My limbs polluted by the clinging mud;
Flowers from the graveyard torn, my wreath appalling;
For ghastly sacrifice hoarse ravens calling,
And for the fragrant incense of my blood. 3

*Headsmen.* Out of the way, gentlemen, out of the way!

Why gaze upon the good man so?
The ax of death soon lays him low.
Yet good men once sought shelter free,
Like birds, upon this kindly tree. 4

Come, Chārudatta, come!

*Chārudatta.* Incalculable are the ways of human destiny, that I am come to such a plight!

Red marks of hands in sandal paste
O'er all my body have been placed;

The man, with meal and powder strewn,
Is now to beast of offering grown. 5

[*He gazes intently before him.*] Alas for human differences! [*Mournfully.*]

For when they see the fate that I must brave,
With tears for death's poor victim freely given,
The citizens cry "shame," yet cannot save,—
Can only pray that I attain to heaven. 6

*Headsmen.* Out of the way, gentlemen, out of the way! Why do you gaze upon him?

God Indra moving through the sky,[1]
The calving cow, the falling star,
The good man when he needs must die,—
These four behold not from afar. 7

*Goha.* Look, Ahīnta! Look, man!

While he, of citizens the best,
Goes to his death at fate's behest,
Does heaven thus weep that he must die?
Does lightning paint the cloudless sky? 8

*Ahīnta.* Goha, man,

The heaven weeps not that he must die,
Nor lightning paints the cloudless sky;
Yet streams are falling constantly
From many a woman's clouded eye. 9

And again:

While this poor victim to his death is led,
No man nor woman here but sorely weeps;
And so the dust, by countless tear-drops fed,
Thus peacefully upon the highway sleeps. 10

*Chārudatta.* [*Gazes intently. Mournfully.*]

These women, in their palaces who stay,
From half-shut windows peering, thus lament,

[1] That is, the lightning.

"Alas for Chārudatta! Woe the day!"
    And pity-streaming eyes on me are bent. 11

*Headsmen.* Come, Chārudatta, come! Here is the place of proclamation. Beat the drum and proclaim the sentence.

Listen, good people, listen! This is the noble Chārudatta, son of Sāgaradatta, and grandson of the merchant Vinayadatta. This malefactor enticed the courtezan Vasantasenā into the deserted old garden Pushpakaranda, and for a mere trifle murdered her by strangling. He was taken with the booty, and confessed his guilt. Therefore are we under orders from King Pālaka to execute him. And if any other commit such a crime, accursèd in this world and the next, him too King Pālaka condemns to the like punishment.

*Chārudatta.* [*Despondently. Aside.*]

By hundred sacrifices purified,
    My radiant name
Was once proclaimed by countless altars' side,
    And knew no blame.
Now comes my hour of death, and evil men
    Of baser fame
In public spots proclaim it once again,
    But linked with shame. 12

[*He looks up and stops his ears.*] Vasantasenā! Oh, my belovèd!

From thy dear lips, that vied with coral's red,
  Betraying teeth more bright than moonbeams fair,
My soul with heaven's nectar once was fed.
How can I, helpless, taste that poison dread,
  To drink shame's poisoned cup how can I bear? 13

*Headsmen.* Out of the way, gentlemen, out of the way!

This treasure-house, with pearls of virtue stored,
  This bridge for good men o'er misfortune's river,
This gem now robbed of all its golden hoard,
  Departs our town to-day, departs forever. 14

And again:

Whom fortune favors, find
That all the world is kind;
Whose happy days are ended,
Are rarely thus befriended. 15

*Chārudatta.* [*Looks about him.*]

Their faces with their garments' hem now hiding,
They stand afar, whom once I counted friends:
Even foes have smiles for men with Fortune biding;
But friends prove faithless when good fortune ends. 16

*Headsmen.* They are out of the way. The street is cleared. Lead on the condemned criminal.

*Chārudatta.* [*Sighing.*]

My friend Maitreya! Oh, this cruel blow!
My wife, thou issue of a spotless strain!
My Rohasena! Here am I, laid low
By sternest fate; and thou, thou dost not know
That all thy childish games are played in vain.
Thou playest, heedless of another's pain! (ix. 29)

*Voices behind the scenes.* My father! Oh, my friend!

*Chārudatta.* [*Listens. Mournfully.*] You are a leader in your own caste. I would beg a favor at your hands.

*Headsmen.* From *our* hands you would receive a favor?

*Chārudatta.* Heaven forbid! Yet a headsman is neither so wanton nor so cruel as King Pālaka. That I may be happy in the other world, I ask to see the face of my son.

*Headsmen.* So be it.

*A voice behind the scenes.* My father! oh, my father! [*Chārudatta hears the words, and mournfully repeats his request.*]

*Headsmen.* Citizens, make way a moment. Let the noble Chārudatta look upon the face of his son. [*Turning to the back of the stage.*] This way, sir! Come on, little boy!

[*Enter Maitreya, with Rohasena.*]

*Maitreya.* Make haste, my boy, make haste! Your father is being led to his death.

*Rohasena.* My father! oh, my father!

*Maitreya.* Oh, my friend! Where must I behold you now?

*Chārudatta.* [*Perceives his son and his friend.*] Alas, my son! Alas, Maitreya! [*Mournfully.*] Ah, woe is me!

Long, too long, shall I thirst in vain
Through all my sojourn dread;
This vessel[1] small will not contain
The water for the dead. 17

What may I give my son? [*He looks at himself, and perceives the sacrificial cord.*] Ah, this at least is mine.

The precious cord that Brahmans hold
Is unadorned with pearls and gold;
Yet, girt therewith, they sacrifice
To gods above and fathers[2] old. 18

[*He gives Rohasena the cord.*]

*Goha.* Come, Chārudatta! Come, man!

*Ahīnta.* Man, do you name the noble Chārudatta's name, and forget the title? Remember:

In happy hours, in death, by night, by day,
Roving as free as a yet unbroken colt,
Fate wanders on her unrestricted way. 19

And again:

Life will depart his body soon;
Shall our reproaches bow his head?
Although eclipse may seize the moon,
We worship while it seems but dead. 20

*Rohasena.* Oh, headsmen, where are you leading my father?

[1] Rohasena is himself conceived as the receptacle of the water which a son must pour as a drink-offering to his dead father. [2] The Manes or spirits of the blessed dead.

*Chārudatta.* My darling,

About my neck I needs must wear
  The oleander-wreath;
Upon my shoulder I must bear
The stake, and in my heart the care
  Of near-approaching death.
I go to-day to meet a dastard's ending,
A victim, at the fatal altar bending. 21

*Goha.* My boy,

Not we the headsmen are,
  Though born of headsman race;
Thy father's life who mar,
  These, these are headsmen base. 22

*Rohasena.* Then why do you murder my father?

*Goha.* Bless you, 't is the king's orders must bear the blame, not we.

*Rohasena.* Kill me, and let father go free.

*Goha.* Bless you, may you live long for saying that!

*Chārudatta.* [*Tearfully embracing his son.*]

This treasure—love—this taste of heaven,
To rich and poor alike is given;
Than sandal better, or than balm,
To soothe the heart and give it calm. 23

About my neck I needs must wear
  The oleander-wreath,
Upon my shoulder I must bear
The stake, and in my heart the care
  Of near-approaching death.
I go to-day to meet a dastard's ending,
A victim, at the fatal altar bending. (21)

[*He looks about. Aside.*]

Their faces with their garments' hem now hiding,
  They stand afar, whom once I counted friends:

Even foes have smiles (16)

*Maitreya.* My good men, let my dear friend Chārudatta go free, and kill me instead.

*Chārudatta.* Heaven forbid! [*He looks about. Aside.*] Now I understand.

for men with Fortune biding;
But friends prove faithless when good fortune ends. (16)

[*Aloud.*] These women, in their palaces who stay,
From half-shut windows peering, thus lament,
"Alas for Chārudatta! Woe the day!"
And pity-streaming eyes on me are bent. (11)

*Goha.* Out of the way, gentlemen, out of the way!

Why gaze upon the good man so,
When shame his living hope lays low?
The cord was broken at the well,
And down the golden pitcher fell. 24

*Chārudatta.* [*Mournfully.*]

From thy dear lips, that vied with coral's red,
Betraying teeth more bright than moonbeams fair,
My soul with heaven's nectar once was fed.
How can I, helpless, taste that poison dread,
To drink shame's poisoned cup how can I bear? (13)

*Ahīnta.* Proclaim the sentence again, man. [*Goha does so.*]

*Chārud.* So lowly fallen! till shame my virtues blur,
Till such an ending seem not loss, but gain!
Yet o'er my heart there creeps a saddening pain,
To hear them cry abroad "*You* murdered *her!*" 25

[*Enter Sthāvaraka, fettered, in the palace tower.*]

*Sthāvaraka.* [*After listening to the proclamation. In distress.*] What! the innocent Chārudatta is being put to death? And my master has thrown me into chains! Well, I must shout to them. —Listen, good gentlemen, listen! It was I, wretch that I am, who carried Vasantasenā to the old garden Pushpakaranda, because she mistook my bullock-cart for another. And then my master, Sansthānaka, found that she would not love him, and it was he, not this gentleman, who murdered her by strangling.—But they are so far away that no one hears me. What shall I do? Shall I cast myself down? [*He reflects.*] If I do, then the noble Chārudatta will not be put to death. Yes, through this broken window I will throw myself down from the palace tower. Better that I should meet my end, than that the noble Chārudatta should perish, this tree of life for noble youths. And if I die in such a cause, I have attained heaven. [*He throws himself down.*] Wonderful! I did not meet my end, and my fetters are broken. So I will follow the sound of the headsmen's voices. [*He discovers the headsmen, and hastens forward.*] Headsmen, headsmen, make way!

*Headsmen.* For whom shall we make way?

*Sthāvaraka.* Listen, good gentlemen, listen! It was I, wretch that I am, who carried Vasantasenā to the old garden Pushpakaranda, because she mistook my bullock-cart for another. And then my master, Sansthānaka, found that she would not love him, and it was he, not this gentleman, who murdered her by strangling.

*Chārudatta.* Thank heaven!

> But who thus gladdens this my latest morn,
> When in Time's snare I struggle all forlorn,
> A streaming cloud above the rainless corn? 26

Listen! do you hear what I say?

> Death have I never feared, but blackened fame;
> My death were welcome, coming free from shame,
> As were a son, new-born to bear my name. 27

And again:

> That small, weak fool, whom I have never hated,
> Stained me with sin wherewith himself was mated,
> An arrow, with most deadly poison baited. 28

*Headsmen.* Are you telling the truth, Sthāvaraka?

*Sthāvaraka.* I am. And to keep me from telling anybody, he cast me into chains, and imprisoned me in the tower of his palace.

[*Enter Sansthānaka.*]

*Sansthānaka.* [*Gleefully.*]

I ate a shour and bitter dish
Of meat and herbs and shoup and fish;
I tried at home my tongue to tickle
With rice-cakes plain, and rice with treacle. 29

[*He listens.*] The headsmen's voices! They shound like a broken brass cymbal. I hear the music of the fatal drum and the kettle-drums, and sho I shuppose that that poor man, Chārudatta, is being led to the place of execution. I musht go and shee it. It is a great delight to shee my enemy die. Beshides, I 've heard that a man who shees his enemy being killed, is sure not to have shore eyes in his next birth. I acted like a worm that had crept into the knot of a lotush-root. I looked for a hole to crawl out at, and brought about the death of thish poor man, Chārudatta. Now I 'll climb up the tower of my own palace, and have a look at my own heroic deeds. [*He does so and looks about.*] Wonderful what a crowd there is, to shee that poor man led to his death! What would it be when an arishtocrat, a big man like me, was being led to his death? [*He gazes.*] Look! There he goes toward the shouth, adorned like a young shteer. But why was the proclamation made near my palace tower, and why was it shtopped? [*He looks about.*] Why, my shlave Sthāvaraka is gone, too. I hope he has n't run away and betrayed the shecret. I musht go and look for him. [*He descends and approaches the crowd.*]

*Sthāvaraka.* [*Discovers him.*] There he comes, good masters!

*Headsmen.* Give way! Make room! And shut the door!
Be silent, and say nothing more!
Here comes a mad bull through the press,
Whose horns are sharp with wickedness. 30

*Sansthānaka.* Come, come, make way! [*He approaches.*] Sthāvaraka, my little shon, my shlave, come, let 's go home.

*Sthāvaraka.* You scoundrel! Are you not content with the murder of Vasantasenā? Must you try now to murder the noble Chārudatta, that tree of life to all who loved him?

*Sansthānaka.* I am beautiful as a pot of jewels. I kill no woman!

*Bystanders.* Oho! *you* murdered her, not the noble Chārudatta.

*Sansthānaka.* Who shays that?

*Bystanders.* [*Pointing to Sthāvaraka.*] This honest man.

*Sansthānaka.* [*Fearfully. Aside.*] Merciful heavens! Why did n't I chain that shlave Sthāvaraka fasht? Why, he was a witnessh of my crime. [*He reflects.*] I 'll do it thish way. [*Aloud.*] Lies, lies, good gentlemen. Why, I caught the shlave shtealing gold, and I pounded him, and murdered him, and put him in chains. He hates me. What he shays can't be true. [*He secretly hands Sthāvaraka a bracelet, and whispers.*] Sthāvaraka, my little shon, my shlave, take thish and shay shomething different.

*Sthāvaraka.* [*Takes it.*] Look, gentlemen, look! Why, he is trying to bribe me with gold.

*Sansthānaka.* [*Snatches the bracelet from him.*] That 's the gold that I put him in chains for. [*Angrily.*] Look here, headsmen! I put him in charge of my gold-chest, and when he turned thief, I murdered him and pounded him. If you don't believe it, jusht look at his back.

*Headsmen.* [*Doing so.*] Yes, yes. When a servant is branded that way, no wonder he tells tales.

*Sthāvaraka.* A curse on slavery! A slave convinces nobody. [*Mournfully.*] Noble Chārudatta, I have no further power. [*He falls at Chārudatta's feet.*]

*Chārudatta.* [*Mournfully.*]

Rise, rise! Kind soul to good men fallen on pain!
Brave friend who lendest such unselfish aid!

Thy greatest toil to save me was in vain,
For fate would not. Thy duty now is paid. 31

*Headsmen.* Beat your servant, master, and drive him away.

*Sansthānaka.* Out of the way, you! [*He drives Sthāvaraka away.*] Come, headsmen, what are you waiting for? Kill him.

*Headsmen.* Kill him yourself, if you are in a hurry.

*Rohasena.* Oh, headsmen, kill me and let father go free.

*Sansthānaka.* Yesh, shon *and* father, kill them both.

*Chārudatta.* This fool might do anything. Go, my son, to your mother.

*Rohasena.* And what should I do then?

*Chārud.* Go with thy mother to a hermitage;
No moment, dear, delay;
Lest of thy father's fault thou reap the wage,
And tread the selfsame way. 32

And you, my friend, go with him.

*Maitreya.* Oh, my friend, have you so known me as to think that I can live without you?

*Chārudatta.* Not so, my friend. Your life is your own. You may not throw it away.

*Maitreya.* [*Aside.*] True. And yet I cannot live apart from my friend. And so, when I have taken the boy to his mother, I will follow my friend even in death. [*Aloud.*] Yes, my friend, I will take him to her at once. [*He embraces Chārudatta, then falls at his feet. Rohasena does the same, weeping.*]

*Sansthānaka.* Look here! Did n't I tell you to kill Chārudatta, and his shon, too? [*At this, Chārudatta betrays fear.*]

*Headsmen.* We have n't any orders from the king to kill Chārudatta, and his son, too. Run away, boy, run away! [*They drive Rohasena away.*] Here is the third place of proclamation. Beat the drum! [*They proclaim the sentence again.*]

*Sansthānaka.* [*Aside.*] But the citizens don't believe it. [*Aloud.*] Chārudatta, you jackanapes, the citizens don't believe it. Shay it with your own tongue, "I murdered Vasantasenā." [*Chārudatta remains silent.*] Look here, headsmen! The man won't shpeak, the jackanapes Chārudatta. Jusht make him shpeak. Beat him a few times with thish ragged bamboo, or with a chain.

*Goha.* [*Raises his arm to strike.*] Come, Chārudatta, speak!

*Chārudatta.* [*Mournfully.*]

> Now am I sunk so deep in sorrow's sea,
>   I know no fear, I know no sadness more;
> Yet even now one flame still tortures me,
>   That men should say I slew whom I adore. 33

[*Sansthānaka repeats his words.*]

*Chārudatta.* Men of my own city!

> A scoundrel I, who bear the blame,
>   Nor seek in heaven to be blest;
> A maid—or goddess—'t is the same—
>   But *he* will say the rest. (ix. 30)

*Sansthānaka.* Killed her!

*Chārudatta.* So be it.

*Goha.* It 's your turn to kill him, man.

*Ahīnta.* No, yours.

*Goha.* Well, let 's reckon it out. [*He does so at great length.*] Well, if it 's my turn to kill him, we will just let it wait a minute.

*Ahīnta.* Why?

*Goha.* Well, when my father was going to heaven, he said to me, "Son Goha, if it 's your turn to kill him, don't kill the sinner too quick."

*Ahīnta.* But why?

*Goha.* "Perhaps," said he, "some good man might give the money to set him free. Perhaps a son might be born to the king, and to celebrate the event, all the prisoners might be set free. Perhaps an elephant might break loose, and the prisoner might escape in the excitement. Perhaps there might be a change of kings, and all the prisoners might be set free."

*Sansthānaka.* What? What? A change of kings?

*Goha.* Well, let 's reckon it out, whose turn it is.

*Sansthānaka.* Oh, come! Kill Chārudatta at once. [*He takes Sthāvaraka, and withdraws a little.*]

*Headsmen.* Noble Chārudatta, it is the king's commandment that bears the blame, not we headsmen. Think then of what you needs must think.

*Chārudatta.*
Though slandered by a cruel fate,
And stained by men of high estate,
If that my virtue yet regarded be,
Then she who dwells with gods above
Or wheresoever else—my love—
By her sweet nature wipe the stain from me! 34

Tell me. Whither would you have me go?

*Goha.* [*Pointing ahead.*] Why, here is the southern burying-ground, and when a criminal sees that, he says good-by to life in a minute. For look!

One half the corpse gaunt jackals rend and shake,
And ply their horrid task;
One half still hangs impaled upon the stake,
Loud laughter's grinning mask. 35

*Chārudatta.* Alas! Ah, woe is me! [*In his agitation he sits down.*]

*Sansthānaka.* I won't go yet. I 'll jusht shee Chārudatta killed. [*He walks about, gazing.*] Well, well! He shat down.

*Goha.* Are you frightened, Chārudatta?

*Chārudatta.* [*Rising hastily.*] Fool!

Death have I never feared, but blackened fame;
My death were welcome, coming free from shame,
As were a son, new-born to bear my name. (27)

*Goha.* Noble Chārudatta, the moon and the sun dwell in the vault of heaven, yet even they are overtaken by disaster. How much more, death-fearing creatures, and men! In this world, one rises only to fall, another falls only to rise again. But from him who has risen and falls, his body drops like a garment. Lay these thoughts to heart, and be strong. [*To Ahīnta.*] Here is the fourth place of proclamation. Let us proclaim the sentence. [*They do so once again.*]

*Chārudatta.* Vasantasenā! Oh, my belovèd!

From thy dear lips, that vied with coral's red,
  Betraying teeth more bright than moonbeams fair,
My soul with heaven's nectar once was fed.
How can I, helpless, taste that poison dread,
  To drink shame's poisoned cup how can I bear? (13)

[*Enter, in great agitation, Vasantasenā and the Buddhist monk.*]

*Monk.* Strange! My monkish life did me yeoman service when it proved necessary to comfort Vasantasenā, so untimely wearied, and to lead her on her way. Sister in Buddha, whither shall I lead you?

*Vasantasenā.* To the noble Chārudatta's house. Revive me with the sight of him, as the night-blooming water-lily is revived by the sight of the moon.

*Monk.* [*Aside.*] By which road shall I enter? [*He reflects.*] The king's highway—I 'll enter by that. Come, sister in Buddha! Here is the king's highway. [*Listening.*] But what is this great tumult that I hear on the king's highway?

*Vasantasenā.* [*Looking before her.*] Why, there is a great crowd of people before us. Pray find out, sir, what it means. All Ujjayinī tips to one side, as if the earth bore an uneven load.

*Goha.* And here is the last place of proclamation. Beat the drum! Proclaim the sentence! [*They do so.*] Now, Chārudatta, wait! Don't be frightened. You will be killed very quickly.

*Chārudatta.* Ye blessèd gods!

*Monk.* [*Listens. In terror.*] Sister in Buddha, Chārudatta is being led to his death for murdering *you.*

*Vasantasenā.* [*In terror.*] Alas! For my wretched sake the noble Chārudatta put to death? Quick, quick! Oh, lead me thither!

*Monk.* Hasten, oh, hasten, sister in Buddha, to comfort the noble Chārudatta while he yet lives. Make way, gentlemen, make way!

*Vasantasenā.* Make way, make way!

*Goha.* Noble Chārudatta, it is the king's commandment that bears the blame. Think then of what you needs must think.

*Chārudatta.* Why waste words?

> Though slandered by a cruel fate,
> And stained by men of high estate,
> If that my virtue yet regarded be,
> Then she who dwells with gods above
> Or wheresoever else—my love—
> By her sweet nature wipe the stain from me! (34)

*Goha.* [*Drawing his sword.*] Noble Chārudatta, lie flat and be quiet. With one stroke we will kill you and send you to heaven. [*Chārudatta does so. Goha raises his arm to strike. The sword falls from his hand.*] What is this?

> I fiercely grasped within my hand
> My thunderbolt-appalling brand;
> Why did it fall upon the sand? 36

But since it did, I conclude that the noble Chārudatta is not to die. Have mercy, O mighty goddess of the Sahya hills! If only Chārudatta might be saved, then hadst thou shown favor to our headsman caste.

*Ahīnta.* Let us do as we were ordered.

*Goha.* Well, let us do it. [*They make ready to impale Chārudatta.*]

*Chārud.* Though slandered by a cruel fate,
And stained by men of high estate,
If that my virtue yet regarded be,
Then she who dwells with gods above
Or wheresoever else—my love—
By her sweet nature wipe the stain from me! (34)

*Monk and Vasantasenā.* [*Perceiving what is being done.*] Good gentlemen! Hold, hold!

*Vasantasenā.* Good gentlemen! I am the wretch for whose sake he is put to death.

*Goha.* [*Perceiving her.*]

Who is the woman with the streaming hair
That smites her shoulder, loosened from its bands?
She loudly calls upon us to forbear,
And hastens hither with uplifted hands. 37

*Vasantasenā.* Oh, Chārudatta! What does it mean? [*She falls on his breast.*]

*Monk.* Oh, Chārudatta! What does it mean? [*He falls at his feet.*]

*Goha.* [*Anxiously withdrawing.*] Vasantasenā?—At least, we did not kill an innocent man.

*Monk.* [*Rising.*] Thank heaven! Chārudatta lives.

*Goha.* And shall live a hundred years!

*Vasantasenā.* [*Joyfully.*] And I too am brought back to life again.

*Goha.* The king is at the place of sacrifice. Let us report to him what has taken place. [*The two headsmen start to go away.*]

*Sansthānaka.* [*Perceives Vasantasenā. In terror.*] Goodnessh! who brought the shlave back to life? Thish is the end of me. Good! I'll run away. [*He runs away.*]

*Goha.* [*Returning.*] Well, did n't we have orders from the king to put the man to death who murdered Vasantasenā? Let us hunt for the king's brother-in-law. [*Exeunt the two headsmen.*

*Chārudatta.* [*In amazement.*]

Who saves me from the uplifted weapon's scorn,
When in Death's jaws I struggled all forlorn,
A streaming cloud above the rainless corn? 38

[*He gazes at her.*]

Is this Vasantasenā's counterfeit?
  Or she herself, from heaven above descended?
Or do I but in madness see my sweet?
  Or has her precious life not yet been ended? 39

Or again: Did she return from heaven,
  That I might rescued be?
Was her form to another given?
  Is this that other she? 40

*Vasantasenā.* [*Rises tearfully and falls at his feet.*] O noble Chārudatta, I am indeed the wretch for whose sake you are fallen upon this unworthy plight.

*Voices behind the scenes.* A miracle, a miracle! Vasantasenā lives. [*The bystanders repeat the words.*]

*Chārudatta.* [*Listens, then rises suddenly, embraces Vasantasenā, and closes his eyes. In a voice trembling with emotion.*] My love! You *are* Vasantasenā!

*Vasantasenā.* That same unhappy woman.

*Chārudatta.* [*Gazes upon her. Joyfully.*] Can it be? Vasantasenā herself? [*In utter happiness.*]

Her bosom bathed in streaming tears,
  When in Death's power I fell,
Whence is she come to slay my fears,
  Like heavenly magic's spell? 41

Vasantasenā! Oh, my belovèd!

Unto my body, whence the life was fleeting,
  And all for thee, thou knewest life to give.
Oh, magic wonderful in lovers' meeting!
  What power besides could make the dead man live? 42

But see, my belovèd!

My blood-red garment seems a bridegroom's cloak,
Death's garland seems to me a bridal wreath;
My love is near.
And marriage music seems the fatal stroke
Of drums that heralded my instant death;
For she is here. 43

*Vasantasenā.* You with your utter kindliness, what can it be that you have done?

*Chārudatta.* My belovèd, he said that I had killed you.

For ancient hatred's sake, my mighty foe,
Hell's victim now, had almost laid me low. 44

*Vasantasenā.* [*Stopping her ears.*] Heaven avert the omen! It was he, the king's brother-in-law, who killed me.

*Chārudatta.* [*Perceiving the monk.*] But who is this?

*Vasantasenā.* When that unworthy wretch had killed me, this worthy man brought me back to life.

*Chārudatta.* Who are you, unselfish friend?

*Monk.* You do not remember me, sir. I am that shampooer, who once was happy to rub your feet. When I fell into the hands of certain gamblers, this sister in Buddha, upon hearing that I had been your servant, bought my freedom with her jewels. Thereupon I grew tired of the gambler's life, and became a Buddhist monk. Now this lady made a mistake in her bullock-cart, and so came to the old garden Pushpakaranda. But when that unworthy wretch learned that she would not love him, he murdered her by strangling. And I found her there.

*Loud voices behind the scenes.*

Unending victory to Shiva be,
Who Daksha's offering foiled;
And victory may Kārttikeya see,
Who Krauncha smote and spoiled;

And victory to Aryaka the king—
His mighty foe he kills—
Far over all the earth's expansive ring,
That earth her joyous flag abroad may fling,
The snowy banner of Kailāsa's hills. 45

[*Enter hurriedly Sharvilaka.*]

*Sharv.* Yes, Pālaka, the royal wretch, I slew,
Anointing Aryaka good king and true;
And now, like sacrificial flowers, I wed
The king's commandment to my bended head,
To give sad Chārudatta life anew. 46

The foe whose powers and friends had fled, he slew,
Consoled and comforted his subjects true;
And earth's broad sovereignty has gladly wed
His power, and bent to him her lowly head,
Who toward his foe plays Indra's part anew. 47

[*He looks before him.*] Ah! There he will be found, where the people are thus gathered together. Oh, that this deed of King Aryaka might be crowned with the rescued life of noble Chārudatta! [*He quickens his steps.*] Make way, you rascals! [*He discovers Chārudatta. Joyfully.*] Is Chārudatta yet living, and Vasantasenā? Truly, our sovereign's wishes are fulfilled.

Now, thanks to heaven, from sorrow's shoreless sea
I see him saved by her he loved, set free
By that sweet bark, that knew her course to steer
With virtue's tackle and with goodness' gear.
He seems the moon, whose light shines clear at last,
When all the sad eclipse is overpast. 48

Yet how shall I approach him, who have so grievously sinned against him? But no! Honesty is always honorable. [*He approaches and folds his hands. Aloud.*] O noble Chārudatta!

*Chārudatta.* Who are you, sir?

*Sharvilaka.* I forced your house in manner base,
And stole the gems there left behind;
But though this sin oppress my mind,
I throw myself upon your grace. 49

*Chārudatta.* Not so, my friend. Thereby you showed your faith in me. [*He embraces him.*]

*Sharvilaka.* And one thing more:
The very noble Aryaka,
To save his family and name,
Has slain the wretched Pālaka,
A victim at the altar's flame. 50

*Chārudatta.* What say you?

*Sharvilaka.* 'T was your cart helped him on his way,
Who sought the shelter of your name;
He slew King Pālaka to-day,
A victim at the altar's flame. 51

*Chārudatta.* Sharvilaka, did you set free that Aryaka, whom Pālaka took from his hamlet, and confined without cause in the tower?

*Sharvilaka.* I did.

*Chārudatta.* This is indeed most welcome tidings.

*Sharvilaka.* Scarcely was your friend Aryaka established in Ujjayinī, when he bestowed upon you the throne of Kushāvatī, on the bank of the Venā. May you graciously receive this first token of his love. [*He turns around.*] Come, lead hither that rascal, that villain, the brother-in-law of the king!

*Voices behind the scenes.* We will, Sharvilaka.

*Sharvilaka.* Sir, King Aryaka declares that he won this kingdom through your virtues, and that you are therefore to have some benefit from it.

*Chārudatta.* The kingdom won through my virtues?

*Voices behind the scenes.* Come on, brother-in-law of the king, and reap the reward of your insolence. [*Enter Sansthānaka, guarded, with his hands tied behind his back.*]

*Sansthānaka.* Goodnessh gracious!

> It came to pass, I ran away
> Like any ass, and had my day.
> They drag me round, a prishoner,
> As if they 'd found a naughty cur. 52

[*He looks about him.*] They crowd around me, though I 'm a relative of the king's. To whom shall I go for help in my helplesshnessh? [*He reflects.*] Good! I 'll go to the man who gives help and shows mercy to the shuppliant. [*He approaches.*] Noble Chārudatta, protect me, protect me! [*He falls at his feet.*]

*Voices behind the scenes.* Noble Chārudatta, leave him to us! let us kill him!

*Sansthānaka.* [*To Chārudatta.*] O helper of the helplessh, protect me!

*Chārudatta.* [*Mercifully.*] Yes, yes. He who seeks protection shall be safe.

*Sharvilaka.* [*Impatiently.*] Confound him! Take him away from Chārudatta! [*To Chārudatta.*] Tell me. What shall be done with the wretch?

> Shall he be bound and dragged until he dies?
> Shall dogs devour the scoundrel as he lies?
> If he should be impaled, 't would be no blunder,
> Nor if we had the rascal sawn asunder. 53

*Chārudatta.* Will you do as I say?

*Sharvilaka.* How can you doubt it?

*Sansthānaka.* Chārudatta! Mashter! I sheek your protection. Protect me, protect me! Do shomething worthy of yourshelf. I 'll never do it again!

*Voices of citizens behind the scenes.* Kill him! Why should the wretch be allowed to live?

[*Vasantasenā takes the garland of death from Chārudatta's neck, and throws it upon Sansthānaka.*]

*Sansthānaka.* You shlave-wench, be merciful, be merciful! I 'll never murder you again. Protect me!

*Sharvilaka.* Come, take him away! Noble Chārudatta, say what shall be done with the wretch.

*Chārudatta.* Will you do as I say?

*Sharvilaka.* How can you doubt it?

*Chārudatta.* Really?

*Sharvilaka.* Really.

*Chārudatta.* Then let him be immediately—

*Sharvilaka.* Killed?

*Chārudatta.* No, no! Set free.

*Sharvilaka.* What for?

*Chārud.* The humbled foe who seeks thine aid,
Thou mayst not smite with steely blade—

*Sharvilaka.* All right. We will have the dogs eat him alive.

*Chārudatta.* No, no!
Be cruelty with kindness paid. 54

*Sharvilaka.* Wonderful! What shall I do? Tell me, sir.

*Chārudatta.* Why, set him free.

*Sharvilaka.* It shall be done.

*Sansthānaka.* Hooray! I breathe again. [*Exit, with the guards.*

*Sharvilaka.* Mistress Vasantasenā, the king is pleased to bestow upon you the title "wedded wife."

*Vasantasenā.* Sir, I desire no more.

*Sharvilaka.* [*Places the veil*[1] *upon Vasantasenā. To Chārudatta.*] Sir, what shall be done for this monk?

*Chārudatta.* Monk, what do you most desire?

*Monk.* When I see this example of the uncertainty of all things,

[1] A token of honorable marriage. Compare page 66.

I am twice content to be a monk.

*Chārudatta.* His purpose is not to be changed, my friend. Let him be appointed spiritual father over all the monasteries in the land.

*Sharvilaka.* It shall be done.

*Monk.* It is all that I desire.

*Vasantasenā.* Now I am indeed brought back to life.

*Sharvilaka.* What shall be done for Sthāvaraka?

*Chārudatta.* Let the good fellow be given his freedom. Let those headsmen be appointed chiefs of all the headsmen. Let Chandanaka be appointed chief of all the police in the land. Let the brother-in-law of the king continue to act exactly as he acted in the past.

*Sharvilaka.* It shall be done. Only *that* man—leave him to me, and I 'll kill him.

*Chārudatta.* He who seeks protection shall be safe.

The humbled foe who seeks thine aid,
Thou mayst not smite with steely blade.
Be cruelty with kindness paid. (54)

*Sharvilaka.* Then tell me what I may yet do for you.

*Chārudatta.* Can there be more than this?

I kept unstained my virtue's even worth,
Granted my enemy his abject suit;
Friend Aryaka destroyed his foeman's root,
And rules a king o'er all the steadfast earth.
This dear-loved maiden is at last mine own,
And you united with me as a friend.
And shall I ask for further mercies, shown
To me, who cannot sound these mercies' end? 58

Fate plays with us like buckets at the well,
Where one is filled, and one an empty shell,
Where one is rising, while another falls;
And shows how life is change—now heaven, now hell. 59

Yet may the wishes of our epilogue be fulfilled.

## EPILOGUE

MAY kine yield streaming milk, the earth her grain,
And may the heaven give never-failing rain,
  The winds waft happiness to all that breathes,
And all that lives, live free from every pain.

In paths of righteousness may Brahmans tread,
And high esteem their high deserving wed;
May kings in justice' ways be ever led,
And earth, submissive, bend her grateful head.

[*Exeunt omnes.*]

# A LIST OF PASSAGES

## IN WHICH THE TRANSLATION DEPARTS FROM PARAB'S TEXT

35.15: Here *nirmitāḥ* is apparently a mere misprint for *nirjitāḥ*.

45.11: The addition of *uṭṭhedha tti* seems almost necessary.

53.10; 54.9; 55.11; 62.7; 66.7: In these passages I have substituted "shampooer" for "gambler," to prevent confusion of the shampooer with the unnamed gambler.

57.13: I have added the stage-direction *dyūtakaramaṇḍalīṁ kṛtvā*.

67.5: Read *kaṁ* for *kiṁ*.

72.9: Read *ajjo bandhuaṇaṁ samassāsiduṁ* for Parab's *ajja bandhuaṇo samassasadu*.

73.5: We should probably read *bīhacchaṁ* (*bībhatsam*) for *vīhatthaṁ*.

87.3: The words *cikitsāṁ kṛtvā* seem to be part of the text, not of the stage-direction.

97.13: I regard *nayasya* as one word, not two (*na yasya*).

100.12: Read *rakṣān* for *rakṣyān*.

114.5: Read *ṇaaraṇārī-* for *ṇaraṇārī-*.

125.8–11: These lines I have omitted.

126.4: Read *accharīa-* (*āçcarya-*) for *accharīdi-*.

170.8: Read *eka-* for *ekā-*.

178.11: Read *vaḍḍhamāṇao* for *vaḍḍhamāṇaa*.

184.9: Read *a* (*ca*) for *ka*.

217.15: Whatever *çavoḍiaṁ* may be, I have translated it in accordance with Lallādīkṣita's gloss, *saveṣṭikam*.

226.2: Apparently *khala-* is a misprint for *khaṇa-*.

238.10: Read *-ruciram* for *-racitam*.

259.16: Read *udvīkṣya* for *udvījya*.

262.4: Read *-bhājanam* for *-bhojanam*.

262.14: Read *paḍicchidaṁ* (*pratīṣṭam*) for *paḍicchiduṁ*.

265.6: Read *tvayā* for *mayā*.

284.14: The words *atha vā* plainly belong to the text, not to the stage-direction.

287.2: I take *paurāḥ* as part of the stage-direction.

288.3–292.9: This passage I have omitted: compare page xii.

# Harvard Oriental Series

EDITED, WITH THE COÖPERATION OF VARIOUS SCHOLARS, BY

CHARLES ROCKWELL LANMAN

PROFESSOR OF SANSKRIT IN HARVARD UNIVERSITY

## Published by Harvard University, Cambridge, Massachusetts

United States of America

⁂ *A copy of any one of these volumes, postage paid, may be obtained directly anywhere within the limits of the Universal Postal Union by sending a Postal Order for the price as given below, to* The Publication Agent of Harvard University, Cambridge, Massachusetts, United States of America.

⁂ *The price per volume of the royal octavos is one dollar and fifty cents ($1.50) = 6 shillings and 2 pence = 6 marks and 27 pfennigs = 7 francs or lire and 70 centimes = 5 kroner and 58 öre = 3 florins and 70 cents Netherlandish. From this, the approximate equivalents of the other prices may be estimated. The precise equivalents may be learned at any post-office that issues money-orders.*

VOLUME I.—The Jātaka-mālā: or Bodhisattva-avadāna-mālā, by Ārya-çūra; edited by HENDRIK KERN, Professor in the University of Leiden, Netherlands. 1891. Royal 8vo, bound in cloth, xiv + 254 pages, price $1.50.

This is the editio princeps of a collection of Buddhist stories in Sanskrit. The text is printed in Nāgarī characters. An English translation of this work, by Professor Speyer, has been published in Professor Max Müller's *Sacred Books of the Buddhists*, London, Henry Frowde, 1895.

VOLUME II.—The Sāṁkhya-pravacana-bhāṣya: or Commentary on the exposition of the Sānkhya philosophy, by Vijñāna-bhikṣu: edited by RICHARD GARBE, Professor in the University of Tübingen. 1895. Royal 8vo, bound in buckram, xiv + 196 pages, price $1.50.

This volume contains the original Sanskrit text of the Sānkhya Aphorisms and of Vijñāna's Commentary, all printed in Roman letters. It is of especial interest in that Vijñāna, not accepting the atheistic doctrine of the original Sānkhya, here comes out as a defender of downright theism. A German translation of the whole work was published by Professor Garbe in the *Abhandlungen für die Kunde des Morgenlandes*, vol. ix., Leipzig, Brockhaus, 1889. "In spite of all the false assumptions and the errors of which Vijñāna-bhikṣu is undoubtedly guilty, his Commentary . . . is after all the one and only work which instructs us concerning many particulars of the doctrines of what is, in my estimation, the most significant system of philosophy that India has produced."—*Editor's Preface.*

VOLUME III.—Buddhism in Translations. By HENRY CLARKE WARREN. 1896. 8vo, buckram, xx + 520 pages, price $1.20.

This is a series of extracts from Pāli writings, done into English, and so arranged as to give a general idea of Ceylonese Buddhism. The work consists of over a hundred selections, comprised in five chapters of about one hundred pages each. Of these, chapters ii., iii., and iv. are on Buddhist doctrine, and concern themselves respectively with the philosophical conceptions that underlie the Buddhist religious system, with the doctrine of Karma and rebirth, and with the scheme of salvation from misery. Chapter i. gives the account of the previous existences of Gotama Buddha and of his life in the last existence up to the attainment of Buddhaship; while the sections of chapter v. are about Buddhist monastic life.

VOLUME IV.—Rāja-çekhara's Karpūra-mañjarī, a drama by the Indian poet Rāja-çekhara (about 900 A.D.): critically edited in the original Prākrit, with a glossarial index and an essay on the life and writings of the poet, by Dr. STEN KONOW, of the University of Christiania, Norway; and translated into English with notes by Professor LANMAN. 1901. Royal 8vo, buckram, xxviii+289 pages, price $1.50.

Here for the first time in the history of Indian philology we have the text of a Prākrit play presented to us in strictly correct Prākrit. Dr. Konow is a pupil of Professor Pischel of Berlin, whose Prākrit grammar has made his authority upon this subject of the very highest. The proofs have had the benefit of Professor Pischel's revision. The importance of the play is primarily linguistic rather than literary.

VOLUMES V. AND VI.—The Bṛhad-Devatā, attributed to Çāunaka, a summary of the deities and myths of the Rig-Veda: critically edited in the original Sanskrit with an introduction and seven appendices, and translated into English with critical and illustrative notes, by ARTHUR A. MACDONELL, Boden Professor of Sanskrit in the University of Oxford, and Fellow of Balliol College. 1904. Royal 8vo, buckram, xxxvi+198 and xvi+334 pages, price per volume $1.50.

Volume V. (or Part I.) contains the introduction and text and appendices. Volume VI. (or Part II.) contains the translation and notes. The arrangement of the material in two volumes is such that the student can have the text of any given passage, together with the translation of that passage and the critical apparatus and the illustrative notes thereto appurtenant, all opened out before his eyes at one time, without having constantly to turn from one part of the volume to another, as is necessary with the usual arrangement of such matter.

VOLUMES VII. AND VIII.—Atharva-Veda Saṁhitā, translated, with a critical and exegetical commentary, by WILLIAM DWIGHT WHITNEY, late Professor of Sanskrit in Yale University. Revised and brought nearer to completion and edited by CHARLES ROCKWELL LANMAN, Professor of Sanskrit in Harvard University. 1905. Royal 8vo, buckram, clxii+1044 (=1206) pages, price of the two volumes $5.00.

This work includes, in the first place, critical notes upon the text, giving the various readings of the manuscripts, and not alone of those collated by Whitney in Europe, but also of those of the apparatus used by S. P. Pandit in the great Bombay edition. Second, the readings of the Paippalāda or Cashmere version, furnished by the late Professor Roth. Further, notice of the corresponding passages in all the other Vedic texts, with report of the various readings. Further, the data of the Hindu scholiast respecting authorship, divinity, and meter of each verse. Also, references to the ancillary literature, especially to the well-edited Kauçika and Vaitāna Sūtras, with account of the ritualistic use therein made of the hymns or parts of hymns, so far as this appears to cast any light upon their meaning. Also, extracts from the printed commentary. And, finally, a simple literal translation, with introduction and indices. Prefixed to the work proper is an elaborate critical and historical introduction.

**Volume IX.**—The Little Clay Cart (Mṛcchakatika), a Hindu drama attributed to King Shūdraka, translated from the original Sanskrit and Prākrits into English prose and verse by Arthur William Ryder, Ph.D., Instructor in Sanskrit in Harvard University. 1905. Royal 8vo, buckram, xxx +177 pages, price $1.50.

**Volume X.**—A Vedic Concordance: being an alphabetic index to every line of every stanza of every hymn of the published Vedic literature, and to every sacrificial and ritual formula thereof. By Maurice Bloomfield, Professor of Sanskrit and Comparative Philology in Johns Hopkins University.

The work, with which Bloomfield has been busy for over a dozen years, will form a royal quarto of about 1100 pages. Of these, fully 800 are already printed (June, 1905); the completely revised manuscript of the remainder is at the press; and it is hoped that the printing will be finished soon after Jan. 1, 1906. For an account of the work, see the last page of vol. iv. of this Series. The Concordance will serve as a register of the *varietas lectionis* for the texts of the Vedic literature, and thus prove to be an auxiliary of the very first importance in the work of making new editions of the Vedic texts; and many subsidiary uses of Bloomfield's collections will suggest themselves to scholars.

## In Preparation

*No promise of a definite time for the completion and appearance of any of the following works will under any circumstances be given; they are nevertheless in such a state of advancement that some public announcement concerning them may properly be made.*

Buddha-ghosa's Way of Purity (*Visuddhi-magga*), a systematic treatise of Buddhist doctrine by Buddha-ghosa (about 400 A.D.): critically edited in the original Pāli by the late Henry Clarke Warren, of Cambridge, Massachusetts.

The "Way of Purity," which has been for fifteen centuries one of the "books of power" in the East, is, as Childers says, "a truly great work, written in terse and lucid language, and showing a marvelous grasp of the subject." Mr. Warren published an elaborate analysis of the entire treatise in the *Journal of the Pāli Text Society for 1891-93*, pages 76-164. His plan was to issue a scholarly edition of the Pāli text of the work, with full but well-sifted critical apparatus, a complete English translation, an index of names, and other useful appendices, and to trace back to their sources all the quotations which Buddha-ghosa constantly makes from the writings of his predecessors. The text, it is hoped, may be published without too much further labor on the part of the editor of the Series.

Mr. Warren died in January, 1899, in the forty-fifth year of his age. Accounts of his life and work may be found in the (New York) *Nation* for Jan. 12, 1899; in the *Harvard Graduates' Magazine* for March, 1899; in the *Journal of the Royal Asiatic Society* for April, 1899 (with a list of his writings); in the (Chicago) *Open Court* for June, 1899; or in the *Journal of the American Oriental Society*, vol. xx., second half.

Buddha-ghosa's Way of Purity, a systematic treatise of Buddhist doctrine, translated into English from the original Pāli of H. C. Warren's edition, by the late Henry Clarke Warren and Charles Rockwell Lanman.

Mr. Warren had made a large part (about one third) of the translation. With this part as a help and guide, the editor of the Series hopes to complete the version and to publish it as soon as is feasible. The text and translation will perhaps take three or four volumes.

## The Pancha-tantra, according to the recension of the Jaina monk Pūrṇa-bhadra (about 1200 A. D.), critically edited in the original Sanskrit by Dr. Johannes Hertel, of the Royal Gymnasium of Doebeln in Saxony, and Dr. Richard Schmidt, of the University of Halle.

The basis of Doctor Schmidt's excellent version of the Pancha-tantra was a text prepared by him from several European manuscripts. In the meantime, Doctor Hertel has procured a very large amount of manuscript material from India, chiefly from Poona, has subjected the same to searching critical study, and is embodying his results, so far as they concern the actual readings, in a thorough revision of the printer's copy of the text. The other results of his labors have been published in several periodicals, especially the *Berichte der Kön. Sächsischen Gesellschaft der Wissenschaften* for April, 1902, and in recent volumes of the *Zeitschrift der Deutschen Morgenländischen Gesellschaft* (lvi., lvii., lviii., lix.). The Çāradā-MS., numbered viii. 145 in the Catalogue of the Deccan College MSS. and containing the Tantra-ākhyāyika or Kashmirian recension of the Pancha-tantra, has proved to be of such great importance for the history of this branch of Sanskrit literature that Doctor Hertel has published it (*Abhandlungen* of the Saxon Society, vol. xxii., 1904), not as a definitive text-edition, but as part of a literary-historical investigation and as one of the essential preliminaries for the edition of Pūrṇa-bhadra's recension to be issued in the Harvard Series. It appears that the last-named recension is a fusion of the Tantra-ākhyāyika and the so-called Textus Simplicior of the Pancha-tantra.

## The Pancha-tantra, translated into English from the original Sanskrit of the recension of Pūrṇa-bhadra, by Paul Elmer More, sometime Assistant in Sanskrit in Harvard University, now of the Editorial Staff of the *New York Evening Post.*

This version, prepared several years ago from Doctor Schmidt's manuscript copy by Mr. More, has yet to be so revised as to bring it into conformity with the meantime thoroughly revised text of Pūrṇa-bhadra's recension. Apart from the intrinsic interest and merit of the stories of which the Pancha-tantra consists, this translation makes an especial appeal to students of Indian antiquities, of folk-lore, and of the history of popular tales.

## History of the Beast-fable of India, with especial reference to the Pancha-tantra and to the related literature of Southwestern Asia and of Medieval Europe, by Dr. Johannes Hertel of the Royal Gymnasium of Doebeln in Saxony.

Although this volume is primarily designed to be an introduction to Pūrṇa-bhadra's Pancha-tantra, its scope is nevertheless such that it may with propriety be entitled a History of the Beast-fable of India. The definitive arrangement of the material is not yet settled, but the general plan may be given under six headings.

I. Brief outline of the incidents of each story, together with a reference for each story to its precise place in the original Sanskrit text, the method of citation to be such that the same reference will apply with equal facility to either the text or the translation or the apparatus criticus or the commentary.

II. Tabular conspectus of strophes and stories contained in forms of the Pancha-tantra anterior to Pūrṇa-bhadra.

III. Apparatus criticus. 1. Account of the MSS. collated. 2. A piece of the text printed in several parallel forms side by side (Tantra-ākhyāyika, Simplicior, Ornatior) as a specimen, to illustrate the relative value of the several MSS. and Pūrṇa-bhadra's way of constructing his recension. 3. Readings of the MSS. Bh, bh, A, P, p, etc.

IV. Introduction to the text of Pūrṇa-bhadra. A. First part, extending to the death, in 1881, of Benfey. 1. Editions: Kosegarten's; Kielhorn-Bühler's; other Indian editions. 2. Translations: of Benfey, Lancereau, Pavolini, Fritze, Galanos. 3. Semitic recensions and their effluxes. 4. Benfey's results as contained in his *Pantschatantra* of 1859 and his Introduction to Bickell's Old Syriac *Kalilag und Damnag* of 1876. B. Second part, from the death of Benfey. 5. Bibliography of the various treatises. 6. History of the Sanskrit Pancha-tantra. Form, age, and name of the original Pancha-tantra. 7. The Brahmanical recensions of the work: Guṇāḍhya, Nepalese fragment, etc.; Tantra-ākhyāyika; Southern Pancha-tantra. 8. Jaina recensions: so-called Simplicior, its age, etc.; so-called Ornatior, author, age, etc.; Megha-vijaya; later recensions; mixed recensions. 9. Buddhist recension, Tantra-ākhyāna.

V. Notes to the several stories of Pūrṇa-bhadra's text. Parallels in the Jātaka, etc. References to Benfey.

VI. Indices. 1. Of names. 2. Of things. 3. Of verses. 4. Of meters.

## The Çakuntalā, a Hindu drama by Kālidāsa: the Bengālī recension critically edited in the original Sanskrit and Prākrits by Richard Pischel, Professor of Sanskrit in the University of Berlin.

Thirty years ago Pischel made his first edition of this master-piece of the Hindu drama. Meantime he has published, as a very important part of the Bühler-Kielhorn *Grundriss der Indo-Arischen Philologie*, his elaborate *Grammatik der Prākrit Sprachen*. In the way of experience and study, therefore, his equipment as an editor of this play is peculiarly complete. As for the externals of paper and print and binding, it is intended that this edition shall be got up in a manner to correspond with its scholarly character and with the intrinsic merit of the play; and it is to be sold at a very moderate price.

## The Çakuntalā, translated into English from the edition of Professor Pischel, with an exegetical and illustrative commentary, by Arthur William Ryder.

Whereas Dr. Ryder's version of The Little Clay Cart (vol. ix. of this Series) was primarily a literary one and aimed to avoid technicalities, his work upon the Çakuntalā is primarily philological, and of it the technical commentary is an essential part. In this comment he hopes to include the most or all that is of substantive importance in the observations of his predecessors whether Occidental or Hindu; to treat the relation of the subject-matter of the play to the older forms thereof as seen in the Epos and the Jātaka; to bring out the double meanings and the various other Hindu "embellishments" of the play; to note the parallelisms in poetic thought or diction or technique between the Çakuntalā and the other works of Kālidāsa and of the Indian literature; to illustrate the allusions to the mythology and antiquities of India by citations translated from the best native authorities; to show, throughout, the relation of this play as a work of art to the Hindu canons of dramaturgy; and at least to assemble the data for the solution of the important critical question whether the Çakuntalā may not have served as the model play upon which the earlier of those canons were based.

## The Commentary (Yoga-bhāshya) on Patañjali's aphorisms of the Yoga philosophy, translated from the original Sanskrit into English, with indices of quotations and of philosophical terms, by Dr. James Haughton Woods, Instructor in Philosophy in Harvard University.

Of the six great philosophical systems of India, we can hardly say that more than two, the Sānkhya and the Vedānta, have been made accessible to Occidental students by translations of authoritative Sanskrit works. For Shankara's Comment on the aphorisms of the Vedānta system, we have Deussen's translation into German and Thibaut's into English. For the Sānkhya, we are indebted to the labors of Wilson and Garbe and Gangānāth Jhā for versions of the Kārikā and of the Tattva-kāumudī. The Yoga system is confessedly next in importance; and the Yoga-bhāshya, ascribed to Vyāsa, is the best and most thorough exposition of its fundamental doctrines. It is also the oldest; Garbe refers it to the seventh century of our era, and the evidence adduced by Takakusu of Tokyo may prove it to be considerably earlier.

In the preparation of his translation, Dr. Woods has had the benefit of Deussen's criticism; and he has revised his work under the oversight of Gangādhara Shāstrin and of his pupils in Benares; and he has constantly consulted Vāchaspatimiçra's sub-comment on the Yoga-bhāshya, and, as occasion required, the Yoga-vārttika of Vijñāna-bhikshu and other works of more modern scholiasts. It is hoped that this work will throw light upon the early history of the Mahā-yāna school of Buddhism.

## The Talavakāra or Jāiminīya Brāhmaṇa of the Sāma Veda: critically edited in the original Sanskrit, with a translation into English, by Hanns Oertel, Professor of Linguistics and Comparative Philology in Yale University.

In 1877, A. C. Burnell brought this Brāhmaṇa to the notice of European scholars. Soon after, he procured manuscripts, and turned them over to Professor Whitney. With the aid of pupils, Whitney made a transliterated copy of one, and himself collated the copy with the others. Since 1891, off and on, Oertel has been at work upon the restoration of the corrupt text of this Brāhmaṇa, and has published considerable parts of it in the *Journal of the American Oriental Society* (vol's xv., xvi., xviii., xix., xxiii., and xxvi.) and elsewhere. It is his intention to add to his translation systematic references to the parallel passages from the other Brāhmaṇas.

# Books for the Study of Indo-Iranian Languages

## (Sanskrit, Prākrit, Pāli, Avestan)

# Literatures, Religions, and Antiquities

## Published by Messrs. Ginn & Company

**Boston, New York, Chicago, and London**

Whitney's Sanskrit Grammar. A Sanskrit Grammar, including both the classical language, and the older dialects, of Veda and Brāhmaṇa. By WILLIAM DWIGHT WHITNEY, [late] Professor of Sanskrit and Comparative Philology in Yale University. Third (reprinted from the second, revised and extended) edition. 1896. 8vo. xxvi + 552 pages. Cloth: Mailing price, $3.20. Paper: $2.90.

Cappeller's Sanskrit-English Dictionary. A Sanskrit-English Dictionary. Based upon the St. Petersburg Lexicons. By CARL CAPPELLER, Professor at the University of Jena. Royal 8vo. Cloth. viii + 672 pages. By mail, $6.25.

Lanman's Sanskrit Reader. A Sanskrit Reader: with Vocabulary and Notes. By CHARLES ROCKWELL LANMAN, Professor of Sanskrit in Harvard University. For use in colleges and for private study. Royal 8vo. *Complete:* Text, Notes, and Vocabulary, xxiv + 405 pages. Cloth: Mailing price, $2.00. *Text* alone, for use in examinations, 106 pages. Cloth: Mailing price, 85 cents. *Notes* alone, viii + 109 pages. Cloth: Mailing price, 85 cents.

This Reader is constructed with special reference to the needs of those who have to use it without a teacher. The text is in Oriental characters. The selections are from the Mahā-bhārata, Hitopadeça, Kathā-sarit-sāgara, Laws of Manu, the Rigveda, the Brāhmaṇas, and the Sūtras. The Sanskrit words of the Notes and Vocabulary are in English letters. The Notes render ample assistance in the interpretation of difficult passages.

Sanskrit Text in English Letters. Parts of Nala and Hitopadeça in English Letters. Prepared by CHARLES R. LANMAN. Royal 8vo. Paper. vi + 44 pages. Mailing price, 30 cents.

The Sanskrit text of the first forty-four pages of Lanman's Reader, reprinted in English characters.

Perry's Sanskrit Primer. A Sanskrit Primer: based on the *Leitfaden für den Elementarcursus des Sanskrit* of Prof. Georg Bühler of Vienna. By EDWARD DELAVAN PERRY, Professor of Greek in Columbia University, New York. 1885. 8vo. xii + 230 pages. Mailing price, $1.60.